SPLASHDOWN

SPLASHDOWN

The Story of
My World Cup Year

CHRIS ASHTON

with Paul Morgan

SIMON &
SCHUSTER

London · New York · Sydney · Toronto · New Delhi

A CBS COMPANY

First published in Great Britain by Simon & Schuster, 2011
A division of Simon & Schuster UK Ltd
A CBS COMPANY

1 3 5 7 9 10 8 6 4 2

Simon & Schuster UK Ltd
1st Floor
222 Gray's Inn Road
London WC1X 8HB

www.simonandschuster.co.uk

Simon & Schuster Australia, Sydney
Simon & Schuster India, New Delhi

A CIP catalogue record for this book
is available from the British Library

ISBN: 978-0-85720-803-3

Typeset by M Rules
Printed and bound by CPI Group (UK) Ltd, Croydon, CR0 4YY

To Kevin Ashton, my dad, for his honesty and integrity, discipline, guidance and unfailing support. Although at times it has been difficult to live up to the high standards he set for me, I hope he would have been proud of my achievements to date, both on and off the pitch.

Contents

SPLASHDOWN

Prologue

Twickenham, 13 November 2010. Courtney Lawes receives the ball 10 metres from his line early in the second half. There's only one thing on my mind, or rather coming out of my mouth. I want the ball and I want it now. In a flash, second-row Courtney – who had two Australians bearing down on him – delivered it like the best inside-centre and I was away, with almost the whole length of the Twickenham pitch ahead of me.

At that stage I wasn't thinking about exactly where I was going and whether I could score. It's all about instinct and my instinct took me down the right wing, past the cover and inside Australia wing Drew Mitchell. But as I got closer to the line and realised I was going to score, one face came into my mind, one face that has been with me since my career began, one man who's been right beside me through the highs and the lows – Kevin Ashton. At the end of my 100-metre run, I dived high and handsome over the line – then looked up to the heavens. I dedicated the try to my father.

Of course he should have been there. He should have been there to see his son, from Wigan of all places, score the greatest try of his career at the home of English rugby in front of 80,000 people. I should have been able to look to my right as I went back to my own half for the restart to see my dad in the crowd.

And when I saw him in the post-match reception, he would have shaken my hand – we never hugged because we're Northern men – and just about mustered, 'Not bad, son.'

He wouldn't have let me get carried away but deep down he would have been thrilled for his lad to score such a try at Twickenham. Though, of course, in dissecting the try he would have explained exactly why the dive was a bad idea. 'If you drop it,' I can hear him saying, 'there'll be trouble.'

Sadly, that telling-off is only in my mind because my dad died a few months earlier, a few months before my proudest moment in the game so far. But it doesn't mean he wasn't there with me and if you ever look at the try again you'll see me look up, glancing to the heavens, in a tribute to my dad.

My dad had been there for every game, so it was hard not being able to share this moment with him. Right from the start he was there . . . When I was about twelve, he would take me out running and just dash off. I had to keep up or I wouldn't find my way home.

Two years before that 2010 Test against Australia, I was at

my lowest ebb in rugby. I was stuck in the second team at Northampton and convinced that I should ditch this union experiment and return to the sport I'd known from a young age – rugby league.

But my father was the reason I didn't quit in those dark days and he should have been there to share in my joy. He'd always been there to help and advise. It wasn't always nice. Sometimes after a game he'd tear into me, though it would be for the right reasons. He was invariably right in what he had to say.

And the shame of it is that I never knew how proud he really was of me. I got some idea a few weeks after he had died when one of my sisters found a diary belonging to him – a diary he had never shown me. It detailed my whole career. From my very first game in league to my England debut in union against France, Dad wrote down his real thoughts on a Monday in his diary.

To my face he'd tell me what I should have done and where I went wrong. Behind the scenes he'd write about his pride in seeing his boy playing rugby for a living.

His diary is full of the things he wanted to say to me but couldn't. He just couldn't bring himself to open up. But I can't tell you what it means to me to know he kept that diary.

It all started when Dad had an operation on his knee. It should have taken him three to four weeks to recover, but it was taking twice that time and, Dad being Dad, he refused to go back to the doctor's. He never wanted the operation in the first place and only agreed to it because the family insisted.

Then things seemed to get worse. On the afternoon of my England debut in Paris, he used my hotel room to have an afternoon sleep. We all thought it was some kind of reaction to his knee. In the end we forced him to go back to hospital.

Something was clearly wrong. For two weeks Dad deteriorated. The doctors thought he had an infection that they couldn't identify. They did loads of tests but nothing showed up until he had a bone marrow test, when they found it was lymphoma. He was obviously upset but said that chemotherapy would make him better. He seemed keen to get on with it.

But three days later the family all stood around his hospital bed and watched the doctors switch his life-support machine off. It was a massive shock to all of us. The fact that he didn't suffer for too long gives me a great deal of comfort.

What I've learned from the passing of my dad is that life is never straightforward. I always thought it was.

1

My Twickenham Debut

The nerves were certainly jangling the first time I walked into the dressing rooms at Twickenham as an England player.

The date will forever be ingrained in my mind – 6 November 2010. It was England v New Zealand at the start of the Autumn Internationals, and games don't come much bigger than that. What a day to make your home England debut.

A lad from Wigan, who started out as a rugby league player and was now about to play in one of the most famous rugby union grounds in the world – it's the stuff dreams are made of.

I say 'first time' at Twickenham but in fact I had walked through the dressing-room doors before, when Northampton played in the EDF Energy Trophy final in 2008. Of course we weren't in the big England dressing room that day but in one of the smaller rooms under Twickenham's West Stand. And after we had beaten Exeter, while most of the lads headed for the reception and the free bar, I sneaked off for a peek into the hallowed room where England got changed.

I remember looking at the plaques with the players' names on and thinking, 'I want my name on there one day, when I play for England.' And while I sat in the stand watching the Leicester–Ospreys match that followed ours, I vowed that one day I would be back there in an England jersey. I watched Shane Williams running around for the Ospreys and thought, 'This is where I want to be and what I want to be: an England rugby player at Twickenham.'

Of course, I didn't get the real Twickenham experience that day – for one thing, the crowd was only about 20,000 for our game – and it didn't prepare me for what was to come later in my career. That time couldn't have come quickly enough for me and a couple of years later I was in the England team hotel in Bagshot, waiting for the side to play New Zealand to be read out.

I had three caps to my name at the start of the 2010–11 season and even though I had played in England's recent win over Australia in Sydney, I was very nervous when I went into the team room with the other thirty-odd players and management to hear the team announcement.

Anyone who knows Martin Johnson won't be surprised to hear that there is no fuss, no drama, when he reveals the

England team to play in a Test match. There isn't much ceremony, as all twenty-two names are revealed at once on an overhead projector. Johnno doesn't let you know if you're playing beforehand, but a coach will normally tell you in advance if you're dropped. It's only fair to give that player prior warning.

Yet as I took a chair next to my Northampton team-mate Ben Foden, I wasn't confident of being selected. So when I saw my name next to the number 14, I wanted to shout 'Yes!' and punch the air, as this was going to be my first England game at Twickenham. But you know there are guys in that room who are gutted not to see their name there, players you have beaten to the shirt. You don't want to offend those who haven't made it.

I exchanged a cheeky glance and a smile with Ben, and even though I was ready to explode with excitement that was the extent of my celebrations.

Once the team is revealed you're sent straight out to train, so it's a case of 'let's go'. On our way out, Ben congratulated me, as did Mark Cueto. We had been training as a team for more than a week at this point so you do have an inkling if you're playing or not.

Funnily enough, I had been given prior warning of my first England cap the previous March when I made my debut against France. Before the crucial team meeting, attack coach Brian Smith had taken Ugo Monye to one side to tell him he wasn't playing and that I would be taking his place.

Splashdown

I get on very well with Ugo and, typical of him, even though he wasn't meant to, the first thing he did was come to shake my hand and wish me good luck. 'What do you mean?' I said. I had no idea I was playing. Mike Ford, our defence coach, spotted this and came over. 'Ugo, what are you doing?' he said. He had a bit of a go at him but it wasn't Ugo's fault. And it didn't spoil the moment for me, so Ugo needn't have worried.

Training is a little different after the team announcement. Players are more relaxed, especially as the big defence session is already out of the way, on the Tuesday. That defence session can be punishing, and ahead of a game against New Zealand it has to be – you must replicate the physicality you'll need at Twickenham.

Mentally that first home Test was difficult in small ways – I didn't know exactly how to behave, such as where to sit on the bus or how to interact with the other players. As the team was still new there were four of us making our first Test start at Twickenham: myself, Ben Youngs, Courtney Lawes and Shontayne Hape.

We also had two players who were born in New Zealand in Shontayne and Dylan Hartley. Not that I see Dyls as a Kiwi because he has lived here so long. When he talks to Kiwis he might put on a bit of a Kiwi accent, but that's as close as it gets. It's a bit different with Shontayne, who I knew from rugby league. I played against him in Wigan–Bradford matches but never when he played for the New Zealand rugby league team. He was a very good league player and it's unusual to see him not only change codes but countries as well. It's the same with Lesley Vainikolo – I found it a strange thing to happen.

However, Shontayne has taken the move really well and the most important thing for England is that DJ Shapes (as we call him) is a world-class player. He couldn't really offer an insight into the All Blacks as New Zealand's league and union set-ups are completely different. The All Blacks completely rule that country.

As always, I roomed with Ben Foden the night before the match. Judging by his nerves, it was as if he was making his first appearance at Twickenham, when in fact he had twice come off the bench there for England, against Italy and Ireland.

All the lads tried to make you feel relaxed, but it wasn't considered as big a deal as when we had to go to Wales at the start of the Six Nations. It was home, a place you didn't need to worry about or get nervous about.

With England we have small group meetings with the coaches and I'm in a group with some of the younger lads like Courtney, Dan Cole and Ben Youngs.

On this occasion we met with the team sports psychologist Gerard Murphy and Johnno. Johnno tried to tell us what he would do, what he always did at Twickenham, and how he found playing at the home of English rugby. And that really helped.

He explained that everyone is different in the way they prepare for games. Some people go nuts, banging their heads against the wall, and then you have people like me and Ben Foden, who like to have a joke. Johnno told us there was no right or wrong way to get ready for your Twickenham debut.

He encouraged us to do it our own way and to be ourselves. 'Don't get too worked up about playing at Twickenham and do exactly what you normally do for your clubs,' he said.

I know some sportsmen are sceptical about sports psychologists but Gerard has been very useful to me since coming into the England squad. At first we all found his session quite hard. He would just tell us to say what we were thinking and we'd all look at each other and wonder what he was going on about.

But now we understand the value of our chats with him. Johnno clearly listens to Gerard as the things we tell him can affect training. Once we give our feedback they do things differently and the coaches listen to what we say. It has opened the group up a little.

Not everyone has the confidence to speak up in a big group so the small groups are an important link between the players and management. Often the younger lads in a team can be forgotten and left without a voice, but that doesn't happen with England – Gerard sees to that. Sometimes you don't feel it's your place to talk but in a small group I find it much easier to say my bit.

After a defeat Gerard will ask us why we felt we lost. It might be because we trained for too long or because training wasn't good enough, and the coaches will take that into account.

Over the years a lot has been said about the aura of the All Blacks, but it just wasn't talked about by us that week. Johnno isn't like that. For him every match is fifteen blokes against fifteen blokes on a piece of grass – simple.

Johnno's been to New Zealand, played for their Under-21 team, and won there with England, so he knows exactly how they work. He's not interested in what's said in newspapers, just what happens in the eighty minutes.

One thing that is different with England is that all your kit is laid out in the dressing room by our kit man Reg (Dave Tennison), and he makes sure there is an almost unending supply of base layers, tops and bottoms. As I don't wear shoulder pads or anything similar (that's for league players), all I really needed in my kit bag was my new boots and a clean gumshield. But it still didn't feel right when we left the Pennyhill Park hotel that morning to have an almost empty kit bag in my hand. So, as we were boarding the team bus, in a fit of nerves I went back to my room and filled my bag with tops, socks, trainers, extra boots – anything I could get my hands on. All of which I was never going to wear.

If Reg had seen this he would have thought I was mad, but at least my bag no longer felt light – which made me feel better. I suppose I was worried my stuff wouldn't be there when I got to the ground.

This was a day of new experiences and that included the bus

journey to the ground. I had played for England in Paris, Perth and Sydney but never at home, so I had no idea what to expect. I've never seen anything like it.

The journey is pretty short from our team hotel in Bagshot. It's around twenty minutes and it's rare for anyone to talk. I like to sit as near the back as possible, whether I'm playing for England or Northampton.

On this journey most people were listening to music or just focusing on what lay ahead. It isn't the time for a laugh and a joke; not even I tried to crack a funny.

I hadn't realised we would receive a police escort, nor anticipated the way fans would cheer us almost every inch of the way once we left the motorway. People were coming out of shops to give us their support, stopping what they were doing to turn round and send us on our way. If we didn't already know it, this was a big day!

It was amazing to experience coming into Twickenham for the first time. When you finally get to the big gates, hundreds of people are leaning over wishing you well – it's pretty humbling and reminds you how much England rugby means to so many people. Everyone wants England to do so well. That is never a burden – as players we love the support we get.

I'm always one of the last off, and I was so nervous on this occasion that I came close to offending Johnno, the man who lifted the World Cup for England in 2003.

I didn't know it but Johnno likes to stand at the front of the bus, shaking the hands of all the players as they get off. But no one told me this and I was so distracted by the fans outside that I walked straight into his outstretched hand. I quickly stepped back to shake his hand but I felt a bit stupid.

As you get off everyone starts cheering and then I met Pete Cross, the huge England fan who follows us everywhere and acts as a bit of a mascot for the team. I didn't know he existed before. He stands there shaking everyone's hand as we head to the dressing rooms.

And before you get in the changing room you see a lady who hands the captain a rose and a letter encouraging the team.

'Who's that lady?' I asked the players when we got into the changing room. 'That's Rose,' they told me.

I didn't quite know what was going on for my first Twickenham cap, but I've read her letters a few times since then and you can tell she means exactly what she writes in there. She's just a fan but has carried out this tradition for years. No one else is allowed into the area where she stands near the dressing rooms. It's just the players, management and her at the doorway. She goes into detail about the game and what we need to do. She means every bit of it and it reinforces to me that we're part of something special, something to really treasure. What a lovely lady and a lovely gesture; she's a part of the tradition of playing for England at Twickenham.

We reached the ground about ninety minutes before kick-off. The huge changing rooms aren't anything like the sort we might encounter in club rugby. They're split into four rooms, and each player is given a changing booth above which is a plaque with their name on it. It was a real thrill to walk in and see my name engraved on the plaque. I couldn't resist running my hand over it. Sitting there waiting for you is your shirt and other kit, a couple of programmes and, usually, a few messages from the coaches.

My messages that day revolved around New Zealand out-side-half Dan Carter, reminding me which foot he kicked with and making sure I remembered that in their recent games the All Blacks had hardly kicked at all, running almost every piece of possession they got. The coaches were preparing us for a similar game from them.

You don't get any choice about where you sit in the dressing room, but most people keep the same seat for every game after their debut. I was sitting between Mike Tindall and Mark Cueto, which is where I have stayed ever since. I don't know if there was a conscious effort to put me between two of the most experienced players, but both of them acted as a calming influence. Cuets helps a lot when I'm preparing for a game, as he has all the experience in the world.

I like that time before the game. It allows some players to get psyched up but I like to read the programme and get more relaxed, as I know I play my best rugby when I'm relaxed – though it's not easy when you're making your Twickenham debut for England.

My locker contains my kit, programmes and my new boots,

which are as pristine as you can imagine. I've never understood people who want to wear in boots or who worry about blisters. For me it's the same every game I play for England – I wear new boots, clean and shiny.

I also can't understand people having dirty boots as they're pretty much the only thing we have to look after. If you were a builder you wouldn't want bent or rusty nails, so why have dirty boots? I like to make an effort to feel and look good.

This is in complete contrast to someone like Ben Foden, who looks like he's done the gardening in his. But he only cleans his car once a year, so that probably explains it!

It does mean I collect quite a few boots over the course of a season. I give away some to charity and some I keep. I still have the ones I wore against Italy and in the home win against Australia.

With my boots sorted and kit arranged, I enjoy the eighty minutes or so that is left before kick-off. It's a chance to chill out and look forward to the game. I flick through the programme and might try to fill in some of the crossword. At Northampton it might be spot the difference or the word search, which is a little easier!

Looking around that impressive dressing room, I gazed into the area where the famous baths are. I gather when they rebuilt the changing rooms that there was a plan to replace the baths with showers, but the players dug their heels in and they were kept. A real Twickenham tradition that the public don't see.

Splashdown

One of my early team-mates at Northampton would throw up about five times before every game. All we could hear was him retching – he didn't feel ready unless he was sick. Fortunately there's no one like that in the England team!

I went out early onto the pitch before the All Blacks game as I wanted to soak up the atmosphere. I tend to go over to the right-hand side to start my warm-up and I was pretty much on my own, as usual.

I did the same things that I've always done, which is running around for five minutes. It's crucial when you play for England that you still keep your club routine, the routine you're used to. So it's the same sprints, the same shuttles, as I do for Northampton. It's my form for Northampton that has got me here, so I need those routines to perform at my best. I remember telling Mike Tindall, 'You must be sick to death of doing this warm-up.' Since his first cap in 2000, he's done exactly the same warm-up every time, and hopefully in ten years' time I'll still find myself doing the same thing at Twickenham.

You shouldn't have the attitude that just because this is England you need to do everything fifty times better – that's not how it works. Stick to what you know, or else you'll end up trying too hard.

Once I'd done a few runs, I did some stretching and then some kicking. Being up on the halfway line allowed me the chance to study the most important player on New Zealand's team, well to me anyway: outside-half Dan Carter. The ten is the man I need to worry about. Where and how he's going to kick. Over the years I've discovered that outside-halves tend to kick in a game exactly the same way they kick in that final warm-up. They're going through their final routines just like me.

When Northampton played Munster in the Heineken Cup the season before, I stood on the halfway line watching Ronan O'Gara banging kicks right in the corner. Perfect spirals every time. And when the game started he carried on banging kicks right into the corner.

From watching the All Blacks in the run-up to this game, we learned they hadn't been kicking the ball at all. They had been running everything, so we knew they were going to do that, and that I wasn't going to have to go back and get too much ball.

I had to think more about how they were going to run the ball back. I had watched video and studied my opposite number, Hosea Gear, but it's not the same until you actually come up against them. Of course I'd know if my opposite wing is right- or left-footed or how he likes to make his breaks, but there's only so much you can learn from a video.

We went back inside. We had the option of wearing Global Positioning System (GPS) devices in this game for the first time after England had been given special dispensation by the International Rugby Board (IRB).

We had been wearing them in training, on our backs, and they were providing some useful information. They track exactly how far and how fast we run in a training session, so a coach can immediately discover how effective the session has been. Their use shows exactly how much work Johnno and his management put into the job.

But like the majority of the team, I had decided against wearing GPS in a match. They're about the size of a small mobile phone, in a pack, and I didn't feel comfortable wearing one in a game. Some players did – Mike Tindall put his on as he was sitting next to me – but I made the decision not to wear it in the days before the game, when we had to sign something saying we were happy if the other lads wore them.

I relished putting my match shirt on. It's embroidered at the bottom with my name, the opposition, the date and the number of caps I've won. Then all twenty-two of us got in a huddle so Johnno could address us. Things were starting to get really serious.

Johnno was in the middle, stomping around as he said his bit. I can't remember half of what he said but he spoke exactly as he would if he was a player. It's what I imagine he would have said if he was the captain and at the end of it he told us to get out there before he ended up putting on a jersey and coming out with us.

Johnno gets himself up for it and it works on the lads in the same way. He knocked the All Blacks down in that team and tried to build us up – a bit of both. The great thing is that he knows exactly what we're about to go through. He told us that people talk about the All Blacks as the best team in the world but that talk doesn't mean anything.

He's faced the haka before, he's played against and beaten New Zealand before, so who better to lead us into this crucial game? At this stage – twenty minutes to go – not much sinks in but tone is important and Johnno got that just right. Upbeat and positive.

From that we go straight out and do the team warm-up. It may look energetic but it isn't too testing for the backs! At that point I could have run all day. We did the same warm-up as we did in the second Test against Australia in Sydney so everyone knew it, which helps us all to fall into it and keeps our minds focused on the job ahead.

I wasn't thinking about the calls and moves as they're already stuck in my head from the preparation we've done in the preceding weeks. I find it pretty easy to remember calls; it's just a matter of learning them. England will change their calls every match sometimes but definitely every series, so it was totally different to how it was the summer before.

Learning the England calls is something you're expected to do in your own time and something you're expected to do well. It's more intense than an exam – if you get them wrong, 80,000 people in the stadium and millions on TV watch you fail. You not only need to learn the calls but make them instinctive. That does take time.

The last messages to me, from Brian Smith and Mike Ford, were to just keep on doing what I've been doing. They reiterated how well it had gone in Australia and that my form for Northampton had brought me into the team, so it was simply about replicating that.

As usual, just before we went out, I washed my gumshield in hot water and went to the toilet. I like to take a minute to gather my thoughts and this time I had a special moment to think about my dad and have a little word with him. His opinion meant a lot to me but now, on one of the biggest days of my life, he wasn't here. He had died a few months earlier. It was strange not to have him there for my first Twickenham cap, but if anything that spurred me on, as it has done every day since we lost him. He was a very special guy and being a rugby union player himself he was always available for advice. I felt he was still alongside me.

Before we ran out, the starting fifteen were pulled into a huddle, with the captain, Lewis Moody, giving us a few words of wisdom before we were ready for the off.

Lewis spoke really well and it helped focus my mind one more time and appreciate the task ahead. It's difficult to give instructions at that stage but, like Johnno, Lewis set the tone. It's a matter of unity and reinforces that you're playing for and with the lads.

Outside the dressing room and into the tunnel there was a real union tradition with the substitutes waiting to cheer us on, clapping the lads out. I never saw that in league.

I remember feeling the heat from the fireworks going off as we ran out and Mike Tindall saying this is exactly what we want and where we all want to be right now. Lewis said these are the days of your life, so remember them.

With only three caps behind me when I ran out that day, not to mention the five-month gap since our last game, it felt a bit like my debut all over again. You do feel unsure in the environment.

And there was something else. Perhaps it was because it was New Zealand waiting for us – the world's number one side – or just because the 2011 World Cup was now less than twelve months away, but you could feel a certain frisson. The players and management weren't sure what to expect. How would we carry on from the summer? Would we build on our great win in Sydney against Australia?

It was time for the anthems. I love standing there and singing the national anthem with my mates. I belt it out. We always try to get the Northampton lads together and I stood between Dylan and Courtney this time. I tend to shut my eyes during the anthem.

I had organised for a number of family and friends to come to the match. My mum Angela, girlfriend Melissa, sisters Claire and Beth and brother David were all there, although I've never been able to pick them out in the crowd, as some players say they can. It may be due to my poor eyesight. When I was young I'd always know where my dad was in the crowd and I'd always try to pick him out – but spotting someone is slightly more difficult with 80,000 people at Twickenham!

Splashdown

After the anthems I just want to get the game started but against New Zealand you must first face up to the haka. The players stand 20 metres apart while the All Blacks do their dance. Like many of our players I hadn't faced the haka before.

Over the years there have been some legendary responses to the haka. Such as Richard Cockerill advancing and going nose-to-nose with Norm Hewitt, or teams turning their backs on them, or David Campese ignoring them by going back near his own posts to do a bit of training. I'd have gladly done what Campese did but there was no one to go with me!

There hadn't been any chat from the players about us doing something to respond to the haka, although I'm up for something like that. I'm keen on making a statement of your own but it doesn't seem anyone else is and to be fair those sort of responses do seem to wind them up more.

England's attitude that day, which came from Johnno, was to let them get on with it. We all knew about the new protocol for the haka, with all teams having to stand behind the 10m line. So we just stood there and watched.

Hosea Gear was also winning his first cap that day. That didn't change anything for me. You could see he was a really good player in a confident team, so it wouldn't make any difference to him. I didn't pick him out in the haka as there was so much going on, so many faces being pulled. The winding-up side of things is probably more for the forwards than a wing like me.

My Twickenham Debut

It was great to be there on the pitch watching but we all appreciated the England fans singing during it, trying to drown it out. It showed they were right behind us. I wanted to join in with their rendition of 'Swing Low, Sweet Chariot'. Again, if someone else had started to, I would have joined in.

I don't think the haka had any effect on me. I didn't need anything else to get up for that game – if anything, it just added to my sense of impatience to get the game started.

The first thirty minutes of the game were a bit of a shock to me, a bit of a reality check after the high of beating Australia in Sydney a few months earlier. It's hard to work out why but we just didn't do any of what we said we were going to do. We started completely the wrong way, and at half-time we were trailing 17–3 with converted tries from Gear and Kieran Read and two penalties from Carter. There was to be no miracle comeback victory from there.

I don't want to make excuses about the way we lost but the All Blacks were coming off a successful Tri Nations, whereas we hadn't played together for six months. Of course we had seen each other in the club environment but it's difficult switching straight from club to Test rugby, if only because of all the calls you have to learn.

It's hard to explain why the switch is so difficult because it's all rugby and you train intensely with the England lads. But until you play there is something missing, and it's only then you feel part of a team. It's the reason why the warm-up games before the World Cup were so important to get our rhythm back. It's okay training together but you don't feel right until you've played that first game together.

Unfortunately that had to be the All Blacks in my first autumn series and it took us thirty minutes to get going in that game, to wake us up and make us realise we probably weren't as good as we thought we were after beating Australia in Sydney the summer before.

That win in June helped me enormously when it came to making my home debut against New Zealand. But I think that for the first half an hour some of us sat back and thought, 'We're playing against New Zealand here and need to be careful about what we're doing.'

We let ourselves down in those first thirty minutes and after the match all I could think about was why that happened. There was a lack of pace and tempo, something we'd had in Australia in June. The fact they came out of the Tri Nations having played a load of games, while we hadn't played in months, was crucial. That can't be an excuse but we weren't up to speed as we were in the summer.

We let them score too many points early on and you can't do that against New Zealand. That's what can happen with a good team but the way we came back to win the second half 13–9 let us know we can actually do it, and gave us the belief that we can beat the All Blacks.

After the game we were all really annoyed but Johnno was calm, repeating that you can't expect to win if you give the All Blacks a head start like that. He said he was happy with the way we rallied and he focused on that. One of the things that defines Johnno's time as England coach is loyalty, and that is a testament to him. Some of the younger lads found it took a while to break into the England team but once you're there he's magnificent at sticking by you through good times and bad.

It would have been easy to make big changes after we lost the first Test of the series in Australia or against New Zealand in November 2010, but he's a firm believer in continuity of selection and that sort of loyalty from a man of his stature is hugely appreciated by the players.

I had a face like thunder in the dressing room but Johnno shook my hand and said well done. Johnno, Brian Smith and Mike Ford all react to losing in exactly the same way as me – we hate it!

I came into the reception to meet my girlfriend Melissa, and one of my closest friends, Ben Lewitt, and I was very annoyed. I'm always angry when we lose but it was worse this time, because the way we came back underlined that the match had been a missed opportunity.

It wasn't a formal dinner afterwards although we sat with our families and other England players. At least we didn't have to share tables with the All Blacks, which used to happen a few years ago. That would have been a nightmare!

I didn't talk to any of the New Zealand players, but straight after the game I had to do a television interview and Dan Carter was right there walking past. He won't remember but

I'll never forget seeing him come round the corner and I went out of my way to offer my hand. He shook it and said well done. I didn't want him to think the defeat was bothering me that much. 'Next time we play you,' I thought, 'I'll remember today and how it felt to be on the losing side.'

After the dinner I was still furious so, although a few of the England players went out for a drink, there was no way I was going to join them. We got dropped off at Pennyhill Park and had the option of staying at the hotel, but I decided to drive straight back to Northampton with Melissa. I had no interest in talking to anyone. I don't know why it is – I suppose I'm a sore loser. There was no cheering me up that night, despite Melissa's best efforts. I don't think we spoke in the ninety-minute journey home. I put on some sad music, which probably made things worse.

I was already thinking about Australia's visit to Twickenham the following weekend. I knew the next few days couldn't go quick enough – if someone had offered me the chance I'd have played against Australia the next day!

When I got home, I put myself through the agony of watching the game again – with my dog, Henry – as it was on Sky Plus. It must be the only way I learn – subconsciously I probably want to make it hurt even more so that I learn from the defeat.

We knew straight after the game that we had lost it in the early stages. Sometimes you have to watch a game to find out why, but not in this instance. Everyone knew what we had done wrong. Were we too up for the game? Certainly we made some stupid mistakes that we needed to learn from.

Ironically I was pretty pleased with how I had played, but that didn't help because ultimately we had lost and the team is the most important thing to me.

The huge difference that night was that there wasn't anyone who would offer me solace or some analysis of the game that could help me. My dad would normally have done that, but he wasn't around now to give me that. My mum and Melissa did try but it just didn't have the same effect as the words of my dad.

I'm sure everyone was down about such a defeat, but perhaps not as much as me. People react differently to losing but that game annoyed me. It was my first England Test at Twickenham and I didn't want it to pan out like that. The only thing I could think of to lift my spirits was to give myself a treat on the way home by stopping at a McDonald's.

My recovery only started the next day when I was able to watch the video and analyse the game with the coaches. 'Roll on next Saturday,' I was thinking, 'and quickly.'

England 16 New Zealand 26

England
Try: Hartley **Con:** Flood **Pens:** Flood 3
B Foden; C Ashton, M Tindall, S Hape, M Cueto; T Flood,
B Youngs; A Sheridan, S Thompson, D Cole, C Lawes,
T Palmer, T Croft, L Moody (capt), N Easter

Replacements: D Armitage for Cueto (68), D Care for Youngs (72), D Wilson for Sheridan (58), D Hartley for Thompson (51), D Attwood for Palmer (64), H Fourie for Moody (66)
Not used: C Hodgson

New Zealand
Tries: Gear, Read **Cons:** Carter 2 **Pens:** Carter 4
M Muliaina; J Rokocoko, SB Williams, M Nonu, H Gear; D Carter, A Mathewson; T Woodcock, K Mealamu, O Franks, B Thorn, S Whitelock, J Kaino, R McCaw (capt), K Read
Replacements: I Toeava for Rokocoko (58), A Ellis for Mathewson (51), J Afoa for Franks (75), A Boric for Whitelock (68)
Not used: H Elliot, L Messam, S Donald

Attendance: 80,350
Referee: Romain Poite (France)

2

Australia and *That* Try

The game against Australia was a crucial game for England, as so much of our future depended on our performance against the Wallabies. We had beaten them the previous June, England's best win in years, and now the rematch came seven days after we had been beaten at home by New Zealand. We all knew that if we were going to take England on to the top table of international rugby this was the game we had to win, or least produce a performance our fans could be proud of.

The try against Australia, which announced me on the international stage, wasn't straightforward, they rarely are – a real team effort. In fact, Australia should have scored just before it all happened as they had the ball so close to our line, but somehow Tom Palmer and Mike Tindall managed to turn the ball over and we were away. Turnover ball is the most precious thing in union and something you hardly ever get in league.

Of course there was nothing in the play-book to fall back on when Ben Youngs picked up the ball from a ruck on his own line and decided it was on. It's true that Ben only threw that outrageous dummy because his kicking option was blocked. Quade Cooper had rushed him to stop him clearing.

It didn't mean Ben had to pass. He could have dummied and then kicked. But running from that deep wasn't a poor second option – it suited the spirit of the team and the way we wanted to play, and when Ben set off I was delighted when he found Courtney of all people. I knew Courtney wouldn't (or couldn't!) kick it.

He isn't your typical second-row as he has great hands and is capable of delivering a pass like a back. But there had been a few times that season, playing for Northampton, when we had been in similar situations close to the try-line and he hadn't given it to me, and I'd ended up chiding him, 'What are you doing?'

But that day Courtney got it perfectly right. Perhaps he remembered the way I shouted at him the last time.

When I got the ball I didn't know it was on. I just thought, 'Go, go and see how far you can get.' I knew it wouldn't have mattered if I'd been tackled as we were behind them and the other lads would have supported me.

I was never going to kick the ball. After what happened in Paris, when I chipped ahead after getting a one-on-one with Clément Poitrenaud instead of taking him on, and blowing the chance of scoring a try, there was no way that was going to happen again.

I was also determined not to risk getting isolated and seeing them turn the ball over, even if cutting inside took the run to longer than 100 metres. You get used to thinking about playing the percentages, taking the option which is best for the team.

Cutting inside, I knew there would be support there. I knew England players would be flooding up on my left-hand side as that is how we had trained a million times before. Mark Cueto had certainly set off to support me. Had I needed him he was there.

I knew Drew Mitchell was quick and presumed he would cut me off, but as I veered inside, to look for support in case I was tackled, I could suddenly sense he was struggling, could feel him dropping off. 'This could be on,' I thought.

It doesn't happen too often that you can score a try from 80 or 90 metres, as scramble defences are usually so good, but this time I knew I'd got round the last defender and that there was no one in front of me. And there is no better feeling than when someone has to try to ankle-tap you and fails – and you get to run in from the 22m line.

I've always seen myself as a wing with 400m type of pace. Jason Robinson had amazing pace over the first few metres –

there's no one I know who can match it – but I'll always back myself over longer distances, which is why I got home that day.

I guess it was the perfect range for me, and to get to run in unopposed in front of all those people was an amazing feeling. So much so that I could easily have got carried away and kept on running out of the stadium like Forrest Gump.

Instead, as I reached the try-line, I marked the moment by touching down with an extravagant dive. This 'swallow' dive was one I was to repeat and it was to become one of the most talked-about features of the subsequent Six Nations. But on the day of the Australia game no one mentioned it. Perhaps because of the dramatic build-up to the try.

Cuets (Mark Cueto), Fodes (Ben Foden) and Dyl (Dylan Hartley) were the first people to reach me after I had touched down and they were going crazy. Come to think of it, I'm not sure how Dyl got there so quickly, given he's a hooker. Jet boots maybe? They were just jumping around, going bananas. If only I could put that feeling in a bottle it would be worth a lot of money.

It was strange. In the run-up to the match I'd such a good feeling about this game. I told Fodes (and he has never let me forget it, regularly taking the mickey) that sometimes I have premonitions before a game. Premonitions that I will score or my team will win, and it happened the night before we played Australia.

I'm not saying I dreamed about scoring a length-of-the-field try, but I sensed I would score against the Wallabies. Don't ask me how but I knew it.

That premonition came back to me in the warm-up. I was thinking, 'What will I do if I score in front of all these people at Twickenham on today of all days?' I tried to visualise the score – scoring a try like I did has been a dream of mine since I was four or five years of age.

Since that day many people have asked whether I had a plan in my mind when Courtney passed me the ball. And I tell them that there is no time for a plan in those situations – only the thought to go as far as I can in the shortest possible time. I have to do what comes naturally, not tense up or put too much pressure on myself.

During a run like that I don't hear any noise. Well, not specific sounds but more like white noise. I know the crowd was going crazy but it seemed like everything was going slowly, which is a good thing. There was no panic in my mind. This is what I had trained for, this sort of chance is what I live for.

It's probably because I'm concentrating so hard on what I need to do that I block the crowd out. You don't acknowledge it as you dare not dream what will happen at the other end, because it never happens like that. No one is supposed to score a 100m try for England at Twickenham against one of the best teams in the world.

I was still a relatively unknown player, so I suppose there were only a handful of people who thought this try was on. No one else was even considering it. Only those who knew me best and had watched me at Northampton believed I could make it all the way.

As a child watching Wigan, I had dreamed about playing for England and scoring a try the full length of the pitch in front of 80,000 people, and there I was doing it. Amazing! It's like one of those things you say to your dad – I'm going to be a singer and have a number one. It's one of those stupid things, but in my case it came true.

I was lucky enough to be the one finishing the try that day but the score was about the team's ethic, the team's spirit and the team's desire to score a try like that. That day the team had the faith in us all being able to play. The confidence might not have been there before then but it is now. Tries like that have given everyone in the England team a boost. Once you've done it once, you know you can do it again.

In the years since England won the World Cup in 2003, they had taken a lot of stick for not playing with the ball, but against Australia we did just that.

We have a structure but the coaches want us to play as they know we can. Fewer and fewer teams are kicking the ball now – New Zealand didn't kick at all the previous weekend.

The try, and the attitude of the whole game, was all about Ben Youngs, our scrum-half, and it showed him at his brilliant best. In the first half he ran out of his twenty-two and that is how we wanted to play. The guy was only twenty-one and new to the England set-up, but he set the tempo and created the mindset to score a try like we did. We had won in Sydney a few months before but this was the day when we started really believing that England could start beating the southern hemisphere superpowers again.

A lot has been made of my style, the off-the-shoulder lines I take, and my first try against Australia showed that. I'll always remember the amazing feeling of scoring my first try at the home of English rugby. It put us in front and it was exactly the sort of try I wanted to score. A support try, being inside the ball-carrier when I received the scoring pass.

I was off my wing on the left near the ruck, and just followed the ball. It went from Tins (Mike Tindall) to Cuets to Crofty (Tom Croft), one inside pass after another, before Crofty popped the ball up to me. Nothing was going to stop me getting over the line – not even if there had been a lorry parked in the way.

From then on the game couldn't have gone any better if I had been writing the script. There was an attitude about the team that day because we felt we had failed miserably the week before against New Zealand, and that we had to prove people wrong. There was a feeling that this was our chance to show the world what we were good at, which was playing the way we played for our clubs.

In rugby league I was a full-back and therefore always in the middle of the pitch. I was told to try and be around the ball. All I wanted to do growing up was score tries and where better to do that than around the ball? There is only one man at the back, so as soon as there's a break it's me against him.

35

Splashdown

I play the game to score tries, so anything I can do to get an edge I'll take it. I grew up watching Shaun Edwards, the current Wales and London Wasps coach, at Wigan, seeing him score so many tries by just pouring through and always being the man inside. Shaun was never the fastest player at Wigan, but he was as good at scoring tries as Martin Offiah. Shaun was nowhere near as good a finisher as Offiah, but just as good a try-scorer.

I've never consciously tried to bring something like this into my game but standing on the terraces at Central Park and seeing Shaun in action, it was always going to sink in. You're seeing all these tries that the amazing Wigan team scored and I was thinking that's what I want to do. Without even thinking about it, you realise you can score tries too by doing it.

Playing on the wing in league used to be seen as a bit of a punishment. One of my old coaches, Ian Millward, used to throw me out on the wing if I had dropped the ball, missed a tackle or just slipped over. He knew I hated it out there because in league you can't get involved.

When I came over to union they put me on the wing, and I didn't want to do it. I don't like standing out there on my own. So they gave me free rein to move off my wing and I realised that this was the game for me – you can go where you want. 'Come looking for work,' they told me and I do, except that I don't see it as work.

Since moving to union it's become apparent to me that a lot

of union players haven't got the hang of the tactic of coming off their wing into the line, or they're just too busy watching what's happening elsewhere. I like to hang around at the back of rucks and wait for a little gap to open up. It's something I've taken from league – waiting for someone to make a break and then getting on the end of it.

The great thing is that I've always had the encouragement since my move from league to do it. From day one at Northampton, I always wanted to score tries, and the coaches have backed me. They wanted me to leave my wing, to go looking for tries.

Even though I'd been doing it from the start in union, in the old National Division One, it only became an issue in the 2011 Six Nations when everyone started putting my performances in the spotlight. 'Have you seen what Chris Ashton is doing?' they'd say.

It offers the team another option. Shane Williams has been doing it for years, popping up everywhere for the Ospreys and Wales. Like Shane, I'm lucky to have the pace to get into those positions and often I overrun the ball. But I believe it's about taking risks for high rewards. I'm gambling on the opportunity arising, or the gap opening. The way I look at it, the more times I gamble, the luckier I get.

It does mean that I might have to gamble five times and see it only come off once. I don't mind that and most people won't see the times I try to join the line and see the ball go the other way, or when I run through our line without receiving the ball.

Splashdown

Those times when it doesn't happen are part of the journey to a try.

At both Northampton and England they've encouraged me to play like this, especially at Northampton where Grayse (former England fly-half Paul Grayson) is the coach I work with the most.

Grayse will have a go at me when I'm not on the wing sometimes, but I want to be in and around the ball all the time. I want to be involved in every single play, every single opportunity there is to score a try.

Against Australia, I was close to a hat-trick, but James O'Connor is quick and he covered it well. Maybe next time. Hopefully, I have another ten years of this ahead of me.

After the game people were going crazy. I turned on my phone to see that I'd been sent about fifty texts but in the changing room I didn't want to focus on it. We'd just beaten Australia back-to-back, after the win in Sydney the June before, and recovered from losing to New Zealand, so the post-match celebrations were 100 per cent about the team.

The feeling in that dressing room is one I want to keep hold of for the rest of my career. No one can take those feelings away and you never know how important they could be when our backs are against the wall.

The changing-room atmosphere after the defeat to New Zealand probably drives me more to do my extras in training, and to get out there when some people might not want to.

Defeats stay in your mind more. But after Australia it was still very special and great for our future.

Obviously the banter was flying around quite quickly as the lads gave me stick for taking all the glory and said that it would change me. But I'm from Wigan, I can't change!

We had won as a team. You can't do anything in rugby on your own. We had done something special as a team and we were so happy because there was a huge relief that we had played the way we wanted to, in a style that suited our game plan.

I loved all the text messages but there was one that stood out. It was from a bloke at Wigan called Jack Rhoden, who had been a scout at the club and who used to talk to my dad a lot about the game.

My dad used to say, 'The cream always comes to the top', and that is exactly what Jack texted me. That was a good moment: to realise that people had started to acknowledge that my move from league to union was working out.

In the selection meeting I'd been pleased to see Dyl come back into the side. I thought he had played well when he came on against New Zealand. Dyl is a great team-mate to have alongside you. He's done a great job as captain at Northampton, taking us not only to the Aviva Premiership semi-finals but also to a Heineken Cup final. For him to be such a great leader at only twenty-five is a testament to him.

He came into the team but that was the only change Johnno made to the starting fifteen, despite the defeat a week earlier.

That sort of loyalty is really appreciated by the players but it isn't blind loyalty.

Back in the summer of 2010 after we had beaten Australia, we had a final tour game in New Zealand against the Maori. Most people outside the squad probably thought the Test team would come home but Johnno kept a number of us, me included, with the squad and we travelled to New Zealand. A year before the World Cup, he wanted us to experience rugby in the country that would host it. Especially those who, like me, hadn't done that before. Now we have this experience to look back on and we knew some of what was to come at the World Cup.

At the time it was hard. I asked if I could go home and see my mum before she went on holiday as it was still only a few weeks since my dad had died. But Ugo (Monye) and Dom Waldouck pulled out with injury, so I ended up playing against the Maori. I found myself a winner against Australia on the Saturday and then playing in New Zealand on the Wednesday. It was a tough situation to be in, but in the month afterwards I came to be grateful for the experience. I'm all the better for being in that situation.

I don't play rugby to be noticed, for the fame that comes with playing for England, but one of the reasons I came over from league was because of how much bigger the game of union was. I wanted to be part of that and I'm so glad it has happened.

Scoring tries will never give me an ego, because of the way

my mum and dad brought me up. Some people believe their press but I never will. I think it's down to the environment you're in as a child. I grew up around the sort of Northern people who keep you grounded.

No one in this England team would ever get carried away with themselves and a lot of credit for that should go to the coaches. They will always bring you back down to earth, especially because at this point this England team hadn't won anything. We'd beaten Australia and lifted the Cook Cup but we hadn't even won a Six Nations title since Johnno won himself a Grand Slam in 2003.

The England coaches never let anyone get ahead of themselves. That's a great thing to have within a group of management. It's very similar at Northampton, and, I believe, at Leicester. Dorian West, one of the coaches at Northampton, is an ex-Leicester man who has tried to bring that mentality to Franklin's Gardens. Getting carried away with success or getting above your station is just not accepted, and nor should it be.

After the game it was a little surreal. I was sitting in the dressing room pinching myself, asking myself, 'Did that really happen?' And a big part of me could only think, 'My dad's not here to see it.'

I score a length-of-the-field try at Twickenham for England as we beat Australia and my dad isn't in the crowd. He was there for every other match I played.

After getting changed, the media team at the RFU had lined

up a lot of interviews for me to do, which is fine – who wouldn't want to carry on talking about it? But before that I was scheduled to appear in the Players' Room, a hospitality area for the Rugby Players' Association (RPA).

Throughout the Autumn Internationals or Six Nations, each player will take it in turns to appear in the Players' Room after the match to talk to the supporters and debrief the game – from the stage – for them. If we've lost, it can be tough but after a day like I'd just enjoyed it was a pleasure.

Four of us sat on the stage and as I walked in I started to absorb the magnitude of what we had done that afternoon as everyone started cheering. As my name was read out, it dawned on me what we had achieved. Before that day many people in that room wouldn't have known who I was. It was incredible for a rugby league lad from Wigan to get an ovation like that at Twickenham.

Supporters were asking me about the try and whether the game could change England – and it did that. The victory gave us belief.

Families aren't normally allowed in the room but Louise Kaiser, who works for the RPA, managed to sneak Melissa, my mum and sisters in at the back, as she recognised what a special day it was for the Ashtons. A lovely touch, and I thank her for that. We have a great players' union in England.

I did my interviews and went round to see my family at the back of the room. They could see that although I was euphoric, there was a part of me that was missing my dad.

The contrast from a week earlier couldn't have greater but my mood was about to change.

We were never going to go mad, as we had to play Samoa seven days later, but I decided to hook up with Melissa, Courtney and his then girlfriend, and Dyl and his girlfriend Jo, and head into nearby Richmond. We ended up in the Gaucho Grill for a steak and a few celebratory drinks.

So we were all heading there on a massive high. But as we were walking out of Twickenham my world came crashing down as Richard Smith, the RFU's lawyer, came up to me and said there was a possibility that I'd be cited for a dangerous spear tackle and might be banned from the next game.

My face dropped and that news changed my whole night. My greatest day in union could have turned out to be one of my worst. It dampened the whole evening as I realised I might not play again in the Autumn Internationals. His opinion was that the tackle wasn't too bad, but he wasn't making the decision. I was stunned as I thought it was a good tackle.

When we went for food we were drinking champagne but I couldn't forget about the possible citing. The restaurant was great but we did make a bit of a mistake when we decided to move on to a popular pub near Richmond Bridge. What were we thinking, on a night after England had played?

It was a bad decision, especially going in there with Courtney, as he sticks out like a sore thumb. Dyl and I might have got away with it but Courtney is too big to go into a pub like that unnoticed, especially as we were still in our matching suits.

It was packed with people straight from the game, so we only survived in there for five minutes as we couldn't get anywhere near the bar. Don't get me wrong: it was great to get the adulation, but we had to abandon the idea and jumped in a cab back to the safety of the team hotel at Bagshot.

It was a great scene at the Pennyhill Park hotel as most of the lads were in the bar and as we walked in we were greeted by piano playing and Tins singing. He's extremely good. He may not be due on *Britain's Got Talent* but he knows a lot of songs, a lot of words, and that puts him ahead of most of us. He was booming out a lot of Take That songs and we spent an hour or two in there, but as I say, we knew we would be playing Samoa the following Saturday so we couldn't go too mad. It's just not the done thing any more.

I'd been looking forward to the Australia game more than New Zealand as I felt so much more comfortable in the England environment. I knew the protocols, I knew the drive in, I knew where I was sitting in the changing room, I knew the routines, I knew I could go to a game with almost nothing in my kit bag, and I generally knew what was happening. I was altogether more at ease with being an England international, playing in front of a packed Twickenham.

There was also pressure on us that day because if we didn't win it would be deemed as another England/Home Nations failure against the southern hemisphere, and we couldn't afford that a year before the World Cup.

Defeat would have meant people – and particularly the media – would have started getting on our backs again. We didn't want that; we knew the way we could play and knew we hadn't done that seven days earlier against New Zealand.

A lot of credit for the win over Australia needs to go to the coaches. It would have been easy for them to make us more negative, but they encouraged us to play an expansive style, and straight from the kick-off that's what we did – a philosophy summed up by my try.

We enjoyed the run-up to the Australia game far more than the build-up to the New Zealand game. There was a want and a need to beat the Wallabies and that was transported into our training that week, which was much crisper and smarter. We knew each other better and it was showing.

We all knew how crucial it was to change what had happened a week before, and to make sure we performed as we did in the second half against New Zealand. The pressure suited us and we carried on from where we left off against the All Blacks. Everyone was the same – they just couldn't wait to get out there and prove we could win and show that we're a good team.

I'll never forget that day – they don't come round too often, do they?

England 35 Australia 18

England

Tries: Ashton 2 **Cons**: Flood 2 **Pens**: Flood 7

B Foden; C Ashton, M Tindall, S Hape, M Cueto; T Flood, B Youngs; A Sheridan, D Hartley, D Cole, C Lawes, T Palmer, T Croft, L Moody (capt), N Easter

Replacements: D Armitage for Tindall (62), C Hodgson for Flood (78), D Care for Youngs (54), D Wilson for Sheridan (67), S Thompson for Hartley (70), S Shaw for Palmer (71), H Fourie for Easter (78)

Australia

Tries: Beale 2 **Con**: O'Connor **Pens**: O'Connor 2

K Beale; J O'Connor, A Ashley-Cooper, M Giteau, D Mitchell; Q Cooper, W Genia; B Robinson, S Moore, B Alexander, M Chisholm, N Sharpe, R Elsom (capt), D Pocock, B McCalman

Replacements: B Barnes for Giteau (59), L Burgess for Genia (48), J Slipper for Robinson (55), D Mumm for Chisholm (57), R Brown for McCalman (58)

Not used: Saia Fainga'a, L Turner

Attendance: 80,002

Referee: Craig Joubert (South Africa)

3

Springboks, Concussion and the Samoans

The mood in the England camp was transformed from seven days before, which just shows what a win can do. When we returned to Bagshot after beating Australia, there was nothing but optimism as we prepared to take on Samoa and South Africa in the space of a week. But we don't like to look too far ahead of ourselves, so no one mentioned South Africa at the time. The coming week was all about getting things right for Samoa.

Having beaten a world power in Australia, the fans and media assumed we would absolutely batter Samoa. The victory had caused a huge amount of euphoria, and tickets for Samoa were selling quicker than ever before, which increased the level of expectation hugely and guaranteed a crowd of more than 70,000.

This is exactly what we wanted. We wanted to raise the expectations and to make our supporters happy. Seven, largely unsuccessful, years had passed since England's World Cup triumph and it was great to be involved when everyone was feeling so upbeat. We wanted to maintain the momentum by recording another good win.

Martin Johnson's first objective was to make sure everyone knew that Samoa was more important than Australia, more important than South Africa or New Zealand, because he knew how easy it would be to undo all our good work. He didn't want us thinking we'd done the hard work and that beating Samoa would be easy – though that was never going to happen.

After beating one of the world's top three sides, it's hard to get yourself as motivated for sides like Samoa, because everyone is telling you that you should thrash them. That mentality shouldn't get into your mind but it does. You have to get your head right because if you're just a few per cent off, a team like Samoa has the firepower to beat you. The key message in the camp was: don't change anything. Do exactly what we did in the week of the Australia game because that worked. Don't lessen the intensity or focus by even one per cent – why would you?

Even though in your head you don't drop off even a fraction, it's easy to do it subconsciously after such a great victory.

The so-called underdogs thrive on an opportunity like that, the chance to take on a side that's on a high from a big win the week before, so as far as we were concerned it was get on guard for a shock. The Samoans were coming to Twickenham with a lot of talent and with nothing to lose – a dangerous combination.

Playing for England is tough because so many nations love to hate the English – we seem to be everyone's old enemy, the team everyone wants to beat. Even if we had lost the past twenty games, England would still be the big scalp. Many have that 'anyone but England' attitude but Samoa are one of the few sides who don't. They didn't seem to trade on the hatred of the English in the run-up to the game. Perhaps it's because so many of their players play alongside us in the Aviva Premiership? Off the pitch they are genuinely nice people. We knew and respected so many of their best players, like Alex (Alesana) Tuilagi and Seilala Mapusua, so perhaps that made a difference to the way they looked at us. Don't get me wrong, we knew they would do everything in their power to smash us into submission, but I felt there was a respect between the two teams that week.

Samoa play some of the hardest rugby, and put in some of the biggest hits, of any nation in the world. In fact, I'd say they run harder and tackle harder than any team I've come across. You underestimate them at your peril.

To stress how hard they hit, all we seemed to see in the run-up to the match was the infamous incident in 2005 when

Splashdown

Mark Cueto was smashed in mid-air by Alex Tuilagi, and Lewis Moody reacted by getting involved in a massive fight with him, leading to both players being sent off. By showing us the footage, the coaches were telling us that Samoa were coming to town. Lewis was the last Englishman to be sent off in a Test and the coaches wanted to make it clear what could happen when we took on this team. Discipline would be crucial.

Our video analysis was very difficult pre-match as there isn't much coverage of Samoa. We could watch the individuals playing for their clubs in England and France but as a team there isn't much around. That meant they were largely an unknown quantity to us, which made them even more dangerous.

And that's one of the things that the game needs to fix. Why don't Samoa and the other Island nations have more Tests at home? Why have England never played a Test in Samoa? As a player I'd love to travel to Samoa to play a Test match. Can you imagine what sort of boost England coming to Apia would have for rugby in Samoa – although they're good enough already!

We knew they would be a hard, physical opposition for at least sixty minutes and although the verdict after the game was that we didn't play that well, I think we did our job well. We knew they would be a pain for an hour and we were proved right, as we trailed 8–6 early in the second half. In the last twenty minutes we did exactly what we needed to do – scored the points and put them away. It was a bit painful to watch but that is what rugby is like sometimes – victory was our only objective.

In a match like this we had to be careful to create our own targets, our own benchmark for success, and not get carried away with either the media or fans expecting us to put a cricket score on the Samoans. We knew that was never going to happen and, as much as we explained that in the days before the game, you could tell no one wanted to listen.

I was frustrated by the perception in the media that our performance wasn't up to scratch because we 'only' won 26–13. Half the Samoan team played in the Aviva Premiership and there were others from the Top 14 in France. Although we were at home, and we should never lose at Twickenham, looking at their line-up I have no idea why people outside the squad and management didn't seem to be happy with the win. This is something I've had to learn as an England player – people seem disappointed if we don't win comfortably every week. Some people feel we just have to turn up to beat a side like Samoa – well, that certainly isn't the attitude among the players and coaches. That sort of attitude shows a lack of respect to the Samoans.

People are so fickle and their opinions can be so up and down that it's tough to stay on an even keel yourself. Don't believe the hype when you win and don't get down with the criticism when you lose – that's the philosophy you learn as an England player.

You can't pay attention to outside opinions, especially in a Test week. We knew we had to be on our mettle because we face these players week in, week out in the Premiership. We could never get sucked into believing we'll win by fifty or sixty points. That is exactly what a team like Samoa would want, so you'd be playing right into their hands with that level of over-confidence.

Looking back, I think we did get sucked into their style of play. They leave 'holes' and you know you shouldn't go for them as they aren't really there, but sometimes it's too tempting. The Samoans entice you into those holes and then smash you and turn the ball over.

Fortunately, we still managed to put them away. And despite the media's take on the match, we were pretty happy with the result, especially as it gave us two wins in a week.

Samoa had a haka as well, the Siva Tau, which is more aggressive than the New Zealand one and ends with them walking towards you. But the tension wasn't as intense as it had been two weeks earlier, and facing the Samoan haka showed me that we have to treat the New Zealand one the same by taking the tension out of the situation as much as possible. We have to get rid of the aura that has developed around New Zealand. People are forever building them up and it doesn't make it any easier to beat them. The All Blacks are just a rugby team and can be beaten by any other team. But New Zealand love it, and they play rugby off that aura. We need to play a part in changing that.

Against Samoa it's about doing a job, and doing it

efficiently. We didn't keep up the tempo of the week before against Australia, but the key thing was that we won. We tried to play in the same way but it's hard to have a 'one-size game plan fits all'. They're a tough, uncompromising rugby nation and they showed that against us.

I enjoy playing against world-class players like Alesana Tuilagi . . . but maybe not every week as he often seems to be running straight at me! He did get the chance to run at me once and it might have been a little bit of a shoulder charge that I used to stop him. It's amazing what you go back to sometimes. When I'm under pressure, I resort to what I learned as a kid in my rugby league days.

In the dressing room after the match, Hendre Fourie, who was making his first start, had to go through a tradition we have whereby a debut player has to sing the team a song. Hendre sang 'Afternoon Delight'.

The post-match dinner at Twickenham was more entertaining than usual as the Samoan lads did one of their traditional dances and songs. One of them had no clothes on at one point, dancing around all these people at what is meant to be quite a formal dinner.

As a team we were very content to be sitting there having won two out of three, although we'd have loved to have beaten New Zealand as well. We obviously go out to win every game, but as a team we didn't set ourselves targets for the Investec Autumn series. There was no number of wins that would signify success – it was just about going from game to game. All that mattered was that it was two wins from three games. I still felt that no one really knew what to expect from us as we had turned in three pretty different performances so far. Some people were starting to think, 'Here we go, we're on our way,' but it was up to us to keep a lid on that.

The dinner gave me the chance to talk to David Lemi, who's had a great career in England with Bristol and Wasps. You avoid discussing the game in these chats afterwards, because it's tough talking to a fellow pro who has just lost.

The contrast between Lemi and Tuilagi, on opposite wings, couldn't be greater. Tuilagi is huge and bases his game on physicality, while Lemi is small and elusive, using brilliant footwork. The Wasps wing is a world-class player who has scored some sensational tries. We could have done with some of those tries a week later when South Africa arrived at Twickenham.

England 26 Samoa 13

England
Tries: Banahan, Croft **Cons**: Flood 2 **Pens**: Flood 4
B Foden; C Ashton, M Banahan, S Hape, M Cueto;
T Flood, B Youngs; A Sheridan, D Hartley, D Wilson,
C Lawes, T Palmer, J Haskell, H Fourie, N Easter (capt)
Replacements: D Armitage for Ashton (75), C Hodgson for
Hape (75), D Care for Youngs (68), S Thompson for
Hartley (56), D Cole for Wilson (56), D Attwood for Lawes
(68), T Croft for Haskell (68)

Springboks, Concussion and the Samoans

Samoa
Tries: P Williams, Otto **Pen:** P Williams
P Williams; D Lemi, G Pisi, S Mapusua, A Tuilagi; T Lavea,
K Fotuali'i; Z Taulafo, M Schwalger (capt), A Perenise,
F Levi, K Thompson, O Treviranus, M Salavea, G Stowers
Replacements: F Otto for Lemi (60), G Williams for Pisi
(68), T Paulo for Schwalger (48), C Johnston for Perenise
(68), J Poluleuligaga for Lavea (67), J Tekori for Thompson
(41), A Aiono for Treviranus (66)

Attendance: 70,553
Referee: P Fitzgibbon (Ireland)

Having won two from three, the expectation levels inside the
squad rose – and taking on South Africa in the final match of the
series we found out exactly where we stood in the world game.

I know we lost because I read about it in the papers the next
day, but it's difficult for me to analyse the game because I was
knocked out early in the match and can't remember much
about it. I remember going into a tackle to stop Victor
Matfield and was told later that my head connected with his
ribs – breaking one – and down I went.

In hindsight, I should have come off as there was no question I was concussed. That was a mistake on my part. It was
daft of me not to come off immediately.

To assess a player in that condition the medical staff will ask
you a number of questions on the pitch, and from your answers

they work out whether you're fit to continue. One of the medical staff said to me: 'Start at 100 and count backwards to 93.'

'I can't do that normally!' I replied.

I heard later that the referee, George Clancy, had said 'Get him off', as I was like Bambi on ice for a few minutes.

The incident occurred in the sixth minute. I saw Matfield standing there and knew he was going to get the ball, so I decided to hit him early. I did that but don't know why it went so wrong. Most people think it was a knock to the head but that wasn't the case. I'm not sure exactly what happened but I think I separated my shoulder or something similar which caused me to pass out straightaway. There was no soreness on my head, so I knew it wasn't that. As I hit him, I believe I cut something off to my brain, which caused the problem. It's still classed as concussion but the impact was in my neck.

A player is the worst person to make a decision at a time like that. I'm never going to say 'I'm coming off' – especially not when I'm playing at Twickenham against the world champions.

For most of the game I had no idea where I was and my contribution was almost non-existent. At one point Toby Flood was shouting at me to get back in the line, and although I could hear him I couldn't really do much to comply. We were running moves but I was out of the back-line. I might as well have been walking the dog for all the use I was to the team.

They didn't take me off because I said I was fine and the medical staff were checking on me throughout the game. The physios at the side of the pitch were asking me if I was okay and they were coming on at every opportunity to check on me. And I kept convincing them that I was okay. At the time I did feel okay, but I just wasn't doing what I normally would, even if I felt like I was.

I kept asking Ben Foden the score and what was happening in the match and he would just tell me the score. He's clueless!

They ended up scoring a try, through Lwazi Mvovo, because I was out of position and then finally I was taken off in the 73rd minute.

Obviously I might have come to my senses and scored another try like I did against Australia. That's certainly what I was thinking – hoping I could make something of the game.

I was too caught up in the occasion to think that I might be doing myself permanent damage. I didn't care about that, all I cared about was trying to help England beat South Africa. All I want to do is play in those games – I don't want to miss out on one minute playing for England.

And it didn't matter that it was England. I would have done exactly the same for Northampton, or playing Under-15s for my first club Orrell St James in Wigan . . . and I'd have probably regretted that too afterwards. That's just how I am. I don't want to let my team down and I want to be out there with my mates.

I didn't enjoy sitting on the bench at Twickenham, after coming off. It was awful seeing my mates out there suffering and not being able to do anything about it.

It began to sink in, as this was the last game of the series, that this team wasn't going to play together for a while and it's not the way we wanted it to end. But I believe we learn a lot more from a day like that than from the victories. And that day we learnt that we must be able to change our game plan during a game and cope with adversity. South Africa's defeat by Scotland the weekend before didn't do us any favours at all, because the Springboks were determined to right the wrongs of that performance in Edinburgh.

As the climax to the series, this was the big one for us, so it was doubly disappointing to lose. We had started to get used to our surroundings at Pennyhill Park and the people who were around us, and we had got used to winning as well. There was a mentality in the squad that we could do what we'd been doing and we would be okay. But the game started and it was clear that wasn't to be.

The root of the defeat was simple – they outmuscled us. And that is a frustrating thing for me to say. England's squad has the physicality to match the South Africans, we know that, and we also knew that's what their game plan would be based around, which made the defeat even harder to take.

We just weren't able to change the game during that match. We had got used to throwing the ball around, and we tried to do that but they killed us and kept on killing us on it. We should have changed our game plan to reflect that but we didn't, so this is one game that we as players must hold up our hands and take the blame for. No blame can be attached to the coaches as we could have changed things on the pitch, and didn't.

Springboks, Concussion and the Samoans

I had seen the game as a real opportunity for us to make a statement to the rest of the world, to build on our victories against Australia and Samoa. And the Springboks were under huge pressure, don't forget. I talked to a South African fan at a dinner some time after the match and he said the Springboks didn't believe they would beat us that day, something I found hard to accept. Maybe that slight inferiority complex helped them?

Afterwards it was like New Zealand all over again. We had fought back so well after losing to the All Blacks to beat Australia and Samoa and there I was again in a losing dressing room – I was devastated.

Mine was one of a few big injuries we picked up that day. Tom Croft broke his shoulder defending his own line and Toby Flood was knocked out, while Charlie Hodgson, who came on to replace him, was playing on one foot. Our changing room resembled a scene from *Casualty*.

Floody didn't even know what day it was. He was worse than me. I remember looking at him in the dressing room and he was in the clouds. I had come to a bit after being sat on the bench but he was out of it completely. I thought I was going to see birds flying around his head, he was that bad.

I tried to convince myself I was coming back to life as we had a big night planned because it was the final game. The team had arranged to visit the Smirnoff Experience, so I was trying to get myself straight for that. It was a depressing England dressing room, but Johnno told us that we should be proud with what we had done over the autumn series, and his words started to pick us up.

Yet I believe the experience of the South Africa defeat gave us a reality check of where we were in relation to the three southern hemisphere superpowers, and how much of a step up it was playing those teams. South Africa won the 2007 World Cup because of their physicality and we had to match that.

The night out after the match was our chance to let off steam after four high-pressure Tests and weeks of intense training. I know we had lost but that was still the right time to go and do it. I tried to convince myself, the coaches and the physios that I would be fine to go into central London but Johnno stepped in and said no. He said that if anything happened to me he would feel responsible so it was a no-goer. I think Melissa was more upset than I was.

It was ironic – I convinced them to leave me on the pitch for most of the match, but I couldn't convince them to let me go out afterwards.

I managed to survive the post-match dinner where Hendre had to go through part two of his England initiation. This involves every new cap having one drink with every other member of the twenty-two-man squad! As you can imagine, that takes some doing, so Hendre had been excused this after his debut against Samoa the week before as we had a match seven days later. Now he had to take his punishment.

I knew I wouldn't be going out but I didn't want Hendre to miss out on one of the twenty-one drinks he had to endure, so

I had mine with him at the dinner. I made him drink about five vodkas in a pint of lager. I had to drink that as well, as you must also drink whatever you're giving the new cap. I had two sips and left as my head was beating.

When I'd made my debut in Paris the previous March, I was pretty close to dying because of my initiation – or at least that's what it felt like. It was only Dylan Hartley who saved me, for which I will be eternally grateful.

In Paris I stayed at the back of the room at the dinner with Dyl, and people kept coming up and having a drink with me. I sang the 'Wham Rap!' on the bus, as is traditional with every new cap. That week I spent hours learning it. I knew it pretty well but about two lines into it I got pelted with anything people could get their hands on. But I carried on, you have to.

With the series over in Twickenham, all that was left was for me to be driven back to Pennyhill Park, with my raging headache, as they wouldn't even trust me to drive.

We don't have an immediate debrief from a set of games like this as we have to be back with our clubs on the Monday, preparing for the next game. You speak to the England coaches on the phone and they'll send you stats and their view of how you played. For me that means feedback from Brian Smith (attack coach) and Mike Ford (defence coach).

They send you the stats first as they like you to look at them, interpret them and come back to them with your view on what happened in the four Tests. They show you the number of missed tackles or dominant tackles you made and you then have to explain those to Fordy. For me we discussed system errors – that is, the number of times I didn't work within the defensive system he has laid down. A typical mistake might be flying out of the line.

There wasn't too much bad news and my debrief went better than I thought it would seeing as we had lost twice. The key for the coaches is that they want you to go away from a series of matches learning a few lessons, so you're better the next time. And that means they want you focusing on issues you might have with England while you're back at your club.

Northampton are great at accommodating this and I may work on some issues I've had with England when I'm back at Franklin's Gardens. I don't show the stats to my Northampton coaches but nine times out of ten it works fine.

I got some stick when I got back to my Northampton training, with people calling me a big-time Charlie. But that's a good thing, the lads bringing you back down to earth – exactly where I want to be!

England 11 South Africa 21

England
Try: Foden **Pens:** Flood 2
B Foden; C Ashton, M Tindall, S Hape, M Cueto; T Flood, B Youngs; A Sheridan, D Hartley, D Cole, C Lawes, T Palmer, T Croft, L Moody (capt), N Easter

Replacements: M Banahan for Ashton (73), C Hodgson for Flood (34), D Care for Youngs (62), S Thompson for Hartley (73), D Wilson for Cole (68), S Shaw for Lawes (68), H Fourie for Croft (22)

South Africa
Tries: Alberts, Mvovo **Con:** M Steyn **Pens:** M Steyn 3
Z Kirchner; G Aplon, F Steyn, J de Villiers, L Mvovo;
M Steyn, R Pienaar; T Mtawarira, B du Plessis, J du Plessis,
B Botha, V Matfield (capt), D Stegmann, J Smith, P Spies
Replacements: A Jacobs for Kirchner (47), P Lambie for
Aplon (80), F Hougaard for de Villiers (68), A Strauss for
B du Plessis (79), CJ van der Linde for J du Plessis (53),
F van der Merwe for Botha (67), W Alberts for Stegmann (48)

Attendance: 80,793
Referee: G Clancy (Ireland)

4

Wales

I knew the Wales game, to kick off the 2011 Six Nations, was going to be different from any other I had played in when the psychological war started some two weeks before we kicked off at the Millennium Stadium.

I was in Portugal in January, as England like to go to the Iberian coast for a warm-weather training camp early in each new year. While we were there news filtered through of a verbal attack by Wales coach Warren Gatland on my Northampton and England team-mate Dylan Hartley.

Dyl, our hooker, is one of my best mates in the game so when Warren singled him out for stick my initial reaction was to question why he would do it. His words caused quite a lot of anger in the England camp.

Wales

Out of the blue Gatland had a go at Dyl's lineout throwing and general personality, saying: 'I saw him [Hartley] go to pieces at Leicester a few weeks ago and again on Saturday night. It just shows people can crack under pressure. It's another case of a Kiwi choking on the big occasion.

'Dylan Hartley always seems to have a lot to say for himself, but we will see what he's got next week. Some of what he said was responsible for Richie Rees being banned for a lengthy period, yet he wasn't prepared to step outside with Gareth Williams when he was invited to do so.'

The England team – just for being English – is used to taking stick in the run-up to a Test match, especially against Wales, but it's unusual for someone to take part in a personal attack.

It's something I'd never do as I think an attack like that will do nothing but inspire the person you're attacking and make them more determined to ram those words straight back down your throat.

And that's exactly what happened with Dyl. He really put his head down in the fortnight before the match against Wales, turning in one of his best performances in an England shirt.

Gatland couldn't have done a better job of making sure that Dylan was going to play well. The attack even made him think twice about having a night out with his mates. Traditionally the trip to Portugal is also a time for us to relax in our own company, but when I invited Dyl out on the final night he turned down the chance. I'm sure he was trying to make sure he left no stone unturned for this game.

Splashdown

I spoke to Dyl about it and it was fazing him. It didn't make him doubt himself, but he wanted to make absolutely sure he was going to be 100 per cent ready to face Wales. He was annoyed about it, as he didn't understand why he'd been singled out for criticism, but his first thought was that he was going to leave nothing to chance in the build-up to the game.

Because we had all heard about it through the media, Martin Johnson pulled us all together in a meeting to tell us what Gatland had said. Johnno told us to use it as motivation. He told us Gatland was picking out Dyl, which showed either that he was scared of what would happen in the game, or that he had no confidence so had to pick on someone.

Unfortunately in this instance that was Dyl – but Gatland had chosen the wrong person. Dyl is the sort of person who'll use that sort of stick as a positive. He loves to prove people wrong so, rather than put him off his game, Gatland's words made him even more determined to have a great game against Wales.

Dyl has had his wild times but since Northampton gave him the captaincy in 2009 it has taken him to an altogether new level as a rugby player.

I remember seeing him sitting with Johnno in Portugal chatting about the issue with Gatland and what they were going to do about it. From then on Dyl made sure he had everything covered and that nothing would go wrong against Wales. You could see it had rattled him and he had no idea why Gatland had picked on him. It was no doubt because of two feisty encounters between Northampton and Cardiff in the Heineken Cup a few weeks before.

Afterwards Gatland explained that he had got bored and was looking to spice things up. I can understand that because sometimes I get bored with the round of media interviews and wonder what would happen if I said something controversial. But you can't do that in a position like the one he's in – especially if you then go and get beaten. Gatland took a chance and I think it went too far.

This match was the one that made me realise that England are the team everyone wants to beat, no matter what our form has been like. It's an odd phenomenon in many ways but I regard it as an honour that people want to beat the English. It shows how much England means in the rugby world.

It became a bit of a theme during the tournament and even the France coach Marc Lièvremont weighed in when we played them, saying how much everyone hates the English.

What it means for a player is that there are no weeks off in an England jersey. Later in the Six Nations, even though Ireland had played badly the week before, they were still ready to play the game of their lives against us.

We'd love to go into tournaments under the radar and just slide up there, surprising a few people. But that's impossible if you're wearing an England jersey. We're the favourites in almost every game we play in, whatever the form we have had coming into a Test match.

Splashdown

I had gone to Portugal in 2010 but that was an entirely different trip. That time I was taken along for the experience and was sent home – with Ben Youngs – on the Tuesday, so that we could be available for our clubs the following weekend.

I had also gone to the area with Wigan on a pre-season trip, but that was entirely different to my time with England. With Wigan it was a far more laid-back affair, with a lot more socialising, and one player running through a patio window. I remember we had to get him back on the plane still bleeding, hiding him from the stewardesses.

This time we were still able to go out for a few beers, as Johnno knows we need to do that to let off steam, but obviously we kept a lid on it as none of us want to do anything that would jeopardise our chances of playing for England.

The current squad is a pretty tight group of lads, all of whom understand their responsibilities. There is no one who is completely loose and who gets carried away.

There's no doubt players have jeopardised their chances of playing for England. You don't want to be that guy who lost his place because of something they might have done off the field. I want to make the papers for my rugby and not for being out too late.

We all know that Johnno is interested in the character of his players and not just their abilities on the field. It's important to have good guys in the squad, as they get on with everyone and make the England camp an easier place to be.

Portugal was a week for all of us to get used to being

England players again. We had spent five weeks or so with our clubs so all the calls and moves in my head were Northampton ones. It takes time to switch into England mode and the trip to Portugal, to prepare for the Six Nations, is crucial for that.

While there we were given a new playbook and a new set of calls, so it wasn't even a case of simply remembering what we did in November. All of that was out the window. We were handed a diary full of notes, new moves and calls, and told to look after it as if our lives depended on it. There's no leaving this playbook in the back of a taxi – as was rumoured to have happened in the past to the Gloucester team!

Leaving your folders around doesn't really happen, as the players or coaches simply wouldn't accept it. They're talking about giving us all iPads so the information could be kept more securely, but that hasn't happened yet.

The calls changed from week to week during the Six Nations so it was a job in itself to keep on top of every move we might use. The previous week's calls would be put in a secure bin, to make sure they didn't get into the hands of someone they shouldn't.

I get all the plays in my book apart from the lineouts, because it's useful for me to try and understand every position. However, when it comes to learning calls I'm a bit like Shaun Edwards in that I'm a doer rather than a reader. I take the plays and calls in when they are on the page but they only really come alive for me when we run them at training. Once I'm on the pitch either watching a move or taking part in it I get it straightaway. Don't get me wrong – I can read. I know some people say I can't but I definitely can!

At training sessions we would run loads of seven-man line-outs, five-man lineouts and other positions like midfield scrums and then come up with plays that would work at these set-pieces.

We had set moves planned for Wales and then we changed those for Italy, France and so on. It would be impossible to create a set of moves for a whole tournament – they have to suit a particular team's strengths and weaknesses.

The England coaches are great at listening to our ideas too and Brian Smith is more than happy to incorporate a move or a plan that has come from one of us, which regularly happens.

We will, of course, study other teams and pinch ideas from them, as everyone does. We used New Zealand or South African moves during the Six Nations.

The team to play Wales was taking shape in Portugal, but one thing we did know was that the side was going to need a new captain as Lewis Moody was one of the players who was going to miss out. He had suffered a knee injury during a Heineken Cup match that was expected to keep him out for six weeks. Alongside him both Tom Croft (shoulder) and Courtney Lawes (knee) were also injured, so removing three vital parts of our pack. But such was the progress that England had made in 2010 that we were able to cope with those losses without panicking.

Was their absence disruptive? If it was, no one mentioned it.

Everyone had complete faith in the guys who came in – Louis Deacon, James Haskell and my Northampton team-mate Tom Wood. Mike Tindall took over as captain, an obvious choice. But it was harsh on Nick Easter, who did the job when Moody missed out against Samoa in November.

Johnno waited until we'd got back to England to announce the team to us, but you had a fair idea from the training of who was in and who was out.

One exception to this was Tom Wood, who was told in Portugal that he was going to make his England debut against Wales, to give him more time to get used to it.

Most England fans would hardly have heard of Tom but that didn't faze him. Or me for that matter, as I knew exactly how good a player he is. If anything, it was the perfect chance to prove himself at the highest level.

Tom is the sort of player who never seems to have a bad game. He's so consistent and level-headed that I knew he would cope well with the step up to Test level, and he proved that he knows exactly how to replicate his club form at international level. His whole world had been thrown upside down the summer before, when he left Worcester and came to Northampton. He is living proof that if you put a good player in a good team they will excel.

The environment we created in 2011 was very welcoming to new players, mainly because the majority of us were inexperienced and could remember what it was like walking into Pennyhill Park for the first time, and how intimidating it could be having team meetings or meals with the England squad.

During the Six Nations the England squad was a pretty easygoing place, with a lot of relaxed people, so it was the perfect place for young players to come into and feel at home straightaway.

I looked forward to meeting up with the rest of the England squad. I know some of that is down to the fact that we were winning, but I still believe there is a great atmosphere in the squad.

I get on very well with the rivals for my position, with Ugo (Monye) and Stretts (David Strettle), even though I know they're doing everything in their power to take my England shirt away from me – I would be doing exactly the same if they were in and I was out.

Stretts is a fellow Northerner and in the England squad a fellow bird of prey when it comes to the try-line. He calls me Kes, the eagle, and I think he looks like a bird of prey – two Northern birds together.

At first it can be a little strange with your rivals as you get a perception of people when you only see them on the opposite side of the pitch in club matches. Matt Banahan is a great example of this. Anyone who doesn't know Banners would think, 'What have we got here?' A massive guy, full of tattoos. When I didn't know him I thought he was a bit of an idiot. But, in fact, Banners is a genuinely nice fella, whose personality doesn't in any way match his outer appearance.

I also didn't get off to a great start with Stretts. He was injured and Johnno came over to me and said, 'Strettle won't be happy as you have taken his room.'

I didn't know Stretts at all then and my only view of him was that he was a guy who fancied himself a bit. I remember going down for my first breakfast in the England camp and I was sitting next to him. I tried to ask him something and thought he had completely blanked me. To this day I don't know if he did it on purpose. But I was sitting there thinking, 'People were exactly right about you, pal ...' but then it dawned on me that he might not have heard me! So while we got off to a bad start we have been firm friends ever since. You can't tell anything by first impressions.

I'm sure people say similar things about me but it's easy to get the wrong impression about people when all you do is play club rugby against them and try to knock lumps out of each other on a regular basis. When you get to know people they usually turn out to be very different from your initial idea about them.

At first with England it was difficult, because when I joined the squad we weren't winning, but nowadays the atmosphere is completely different – everyone is happy in each other's company.

Any chance that we were going to arrive in Wales without too much commotion went out the window when Fodes gave an interview to the *Daily Mail* in which he said: 'I'm ready for the most intense experience of my career in Cardiff. All the home nations raise their game against England and are desperate to beat us, but this fixture has an extra edge because our rivalry with the Welsh runs deeply. In a way, we have to think: "We are England, we are the big country, we are going to put these guys in their place." It feels like we are the older brother and we have to make sure we beat our younger brother.'

Fodes couldn't understand the fuss of course. 'What's wrong with it?' he said to me. Sometimes he has no idea! The furore afterwards didn't bother him.

Some of the England players were winding him up, saying, 'What did you say that for?', but England's media team had approved the article and so no one had a real problem with it. And as it was published so close to the game we had more important things on our minds.

Apart from that the build-up was good. Most of us hadn't played at the Millennium Stadium before and Johnno kept telling us there was no better place to play rugby. The passion, fervour and atmosphere in Cardiff is legendary.

We knew that kicking off the Six Nations in Wales was a big ask and Johnno didn't try to play that down. He kept telling us that they hate us and that's the way it was going to be in the match. He prepared us for eighty minutes in which we would be getting a lot of stick from 70,000 passionate rugby fans.

Johnno's words excited me and made me want to play there sooner. The only drawback was that the match was on a Friday evening, so I knew the day would drag out. I wanted to get out there straightaway, and experience it for myself.

Wales

A lot of people were talking about this match as the crucial one, the game that would decide which way the tournament would go for us, and in the end that was proved to be the case as our win over Wales put us on the road to the title.

That expectation meant there was a lot of pressure on us, and as there were two weeks to prepare, one in Portugal and one in Surrey, that increased the tension and made it a lot worse.

We travelled down to Wales by coach on the Thursday, staying one night in the St David's Hotel on the new marina. The night before a match the England set-up are totally relaxed about you having your partners to stay in the room with you. This time, though, I took that a stage further by having not only my girlfriend Melissa stay with me but also my mum. Mum was on the camp bed and she said it was her most uncomfortable night's sleep ever!

I was impressed by how friendly the people were in Cardiff, nothing like Johnno had prepared us for, although that did change once the match started. One year I gather a fan head-butted the England team bus, knocking himself out, but there was nothing like that this time.

Just as I had feared, the Friday dragged and I was delighted to have Melissa there with me so we could get away from it all, with some lunch near the hotel. It's tough to fill those long hours from when you wake until a night match.

The England management are happy for us to eat whatever we want on a match day so we found a YO! Sushi restaurant, one of my favourites, and in keeping with the rest of the people we met the manager insisted on us not paying, which I thought was a lovely gesture. Obviously I'd never tuck into something like fish and chips before a match but sushi is a pretty healthy option and made me feel better, settling a few of my nerves.

At lunch we talked about anything but the match. Melissa isn't a rugby fan (except when it comes to supporting Northampton or England!) and that is great, she helps me get away from rugby.

Stuck in a hotel room looking at four walls isn't for me any day, let alone on an occasion like facing Wales at the start of the Six Nations.

The priority for me on a match day is to be relaxed. With a 7.45pm kick-off I started to prepare for the game at about 4pm, so Melissa and Mum headed for the stadium and left me in my room.

I never realised how stressed I get before a game in that last hour before we need to get our bags on the bus, but it's something Mum and Melissa pointed out, so I know it's something I need to work on. I get quieter and am not my usual self. I know some people get nervous the day before, so I suppose I should count myself lucky it doesn't happen to me until a couple of hours before.

Driving into the ground, it was dark already and we could see thousands of people in the pubs and restaurants around the city. Cardiff is almost unique in the sense that the stadium is right in the middle of the city centre, which brings a special atmosphere. And of course when people realised it was us there was a lot of jeering. Largely good-natured, of course . . .

I have my earphones in on the bus so although I can see the fans I will largely ignore them – on the way to a game, things outside the bus flow over you. The match, and what's going to happen in those eighty minutes to come, is far more important than anything going on around the bus.

I like to feel relaxed on journeys to the game. I know some players are starting to get more aggressive and psyched up, but that has never worked for me. I find I play better if I'm relaxed and happy.

On the way to the game I listen to everything and anything. That day it was a lot of dance music, with a bit of Bob Dylan thrown in. I don't put together a special playlist for a match day – it's just anything I fancy listening to. Almost everyone had their headphones on and I don't remember anyone talking – it was getting serious.

On this journey I was sitting next to James Haskell, and even though he is one of the most chatty guys in the squad we didn't talk. What we were about to do was more important than exchanging pleasantries and that is understood by everyone.

I was focusing on playing better than my opposite number, Shane Williams. I wanted to focus on the positives in those hours before the game. I would never think about things going wrong, like dropping the ball – that's the wrong way to approach a game.

Splashdown

One thing I've discussed with Paul Grayson at North-ampton is that as soon as I start thinking about scoring tries it all starts to go wrong for me and I don't score any. Running around looking to score tries is not how I play and it's not how I get the most out of a game. That can distract me. That night I was focusing on just playing well, as I knew that if I did that the tries would come naturally.

I would be coming up against Shane and a number of people had mentioned that in the run-up to the game. The guy has done so much for Wales, scoring more than fifty Test tries and being named IRB Player of the Year in 2008, and I wanted to be able to compare myself with players like that, world-class players.

I was particularly looking forward to playing against him because I wanted to know how I would cope against a world-class performer. I had to make sure I did everything as well as I possibly could.

Another contentious issue in the hours before kick-off was whether the roof would be open or closed for the game. The Millennium Stadium is one of the few venues in the world with a retractable roof so both sides have to decide if they want it open or not.

Johnno eventually asked our captain Mike Tindall if he wanted it closed or not and Tins said shut, so the match would be protected from the elements, and we went with that.

It did mean that the noise created by the supporters would be even louder. You could see that as a negative as most of the fans were Welsh, but the noise isn't something you pay that much attention to. You're not there for that, you're there to win a Test match. If anything, making it louder was a bonus. It increased the atmosphere and who wouldn't want that? With the roof closed, the Millennium Stadium is an even greater place to play in.

Coming into the dressing-room area I was struck by how many pictures, both paintings and action photos, there are of the Welsh players on the walls. I gather a few years ago they put cardboard cut-outs of the players in the dressing room. There was none of that this time but everywhere you looked on the way in there seemed to be another picture of a Welsh player.

I have seen a few tricks down the years. Traditionally the home changing room is far better than the away one, which it is at Twickenham, and when I played for Wigan a few teams used to paint their away dressing room the day before the match so that when we got there it stank!

Playing for Northampton, we don't get many games when the whole crowd is booing you when you run out, like they did in Cardiff. The only exception is Munster. When I played at Thomond Park with Northampton it was the loudest crowd I'd ever heard. There may only have been 26,000 of them but they made enough noise for triple that. It wasn't louder than the Millennium Stadium, but for that few people it was an outstanding noise.

When we got out on the pitch in Cardiff for our warm-up

it quickly became apparent that we weren't going to be able to hear other players making calls. While we warmed up you could hardly hear what the guy standing next to you was saying, with the crowd jabbering and the band playing.

We had to sprint over to each other and shout. It did have an effect in terms of the calls and we'd talked about it before the game as we knew we'd have to be strong on the calls. When the boys all came in for the huddle on the pitch, Toby Flood was shouting at the top of his voice just to be heard by guys standing a couple of feet away from him. Fortunately, we had been practising those calls for two weeks so we only needed a small indication to know what we were doing.

When I was growing up I didn't know what the Five Nations (as it was called then) was but my dad always used to make me sit and watch the matches on the BBC. He particularly used to make me listen to the noise the crowd made when the Welsh national anthem was sung. He obviously believed even then that I would one day be in the stadium listening to that noise and wanted me to be prepared for it from a young age.

So the anthem was something I appreciated. There I was, standing near the halfway line, and those days in front of the television with my dad helped me prepare for it. It seemed every single Wales fan in the 74,000 crowd was singing that song. But because I knew it was coming, and the playing of the anthem helped me remember my dad, I could enjoy it, rather than be intimidated by it, as I'm sure many opposition players have been in the past.

Wales

It was something I had wanted to experience since I was a small boy and it was as good as I had imagined. I also made sure I sang our anthem twice as loudly as well.

All the nerves were settled so quickly as we made the perfect start, by scoring inside the first fifteen minutes.

The emphasis all week, and the words Johnno left us with in the changing room, were all about starting well. He knows better than anyone how difficult it is for an English team to win in Cardiff if they start badly, if they get behind.

But luckily we were first to score, which allowed us to put some doubt in their mind. I was off my wing, lingering behind a ruck, and saw Toby Flood suddenly have a huge mismatch, somehow being faced by their two props. That wasn't supposed to happen and I'm sure they knew what was coming.

I knew he would break through the line and I was almost there before him, running ahead of the ball. So in a flash it's Floody, me on his inside and only the full-back to beat, which should mean only one thing, and it did – a try. I was screaming my head off but he had to give it to me and he duly did. I was there to take his pass and go over under the posts.

To score the first try of the Six Nations, after an incredible build-up to the game and everything that came with it, was a pretty special moment in my career.

I had no intention of diving but needed to do something to show how much it meant to me, so my brain decided to make the rest of my body dive! That's all it was. It was a jump of excitement and a burst of energy to acknowledge an incredible moment in my career – the scoring of such an important try.

I heard afterwards that on the BBC commentary Brian Moore said: 'One day he'll drop one of those' – we'll see.

I took a lot of stick but that is how I run with the ball anyway, so I'd like to think I had control of it. We even had coaching tips about diving over the try-line. I think they were all right about it because I scored, but if I had dropped it I would have been in a whole world of pain.

It did happen once, when I was playing for Northampton at Edinburgh in the Heineken Cup. I didn't dive, though. Well . . . maybe it was a little bit of a dive! It was the first time it had happened. It was close to the line and someone hit me as I went over and I dropped the ball. I won't let that happen again.

Once I had landed on the turf I got up and looked for the nearest player to celebrate with and of course it was Floody. Now you must understand that Floody plays at Leicester, where celebrating after a try isn't such a big thing, so he proceeded to walk straight past me. I turned to give him a high five and he just looked at me. He had no interest in that whatsoever, and I remember watching it with him afterwards and he was laughing his head off.

One thing you also have to remember is that it is Floody's job to take the conversions so once someone has scored he needs to get the ball and try to kick the extra two points. So when someone scores and smashes the ball into the crowd, Floody has to troop off, retrieve the ball and kick it.

Wales

So on this occasion he ran past me to get the ball. That's his job, plain and simple. 'I'm not bothered, I just want to get the ball and do my job,' he told me afterwards.

He said that I had thrown the ball to the side after scoring which annoyed him more and probably led to him snubbing my high five. That's Floody and Leicester for you, that's how they are!

The other lads soon arrived and we started celebrating, which is lucky as otherwise I might have been left on my own with 70,000 Wales fans.

But before that first try I managed to incur the wrath of a few of the Wales players. By accident.

One of the first things that happened was that we had the ball in our own twenty-two. Earlier in the week we had decided that instead of kicking it we were going to go early, go wide, and catch Wales napping.

I had come in from the left and it was just me, their winger and Ben Foden, but as I passed it to Fodes I saw Stephen Jones come flying up out of nowhere. He smashed into Fodes and it was pretty clear Stephen had come out of it the worst. So when I cleared out the ensuing ruck I remember cheering, not because of what had happened to Stephen but because Fodes had come out on top. I didn't realise Stephen was knocked out – I was just celebrating because it was good for Fodes to knock him back like that, especially at the start of the match.

Not the best thing to do, I realise now, as a couple of the

Splashdown

Welsh forwards took exception to my over-exuberance and tried to get stuck into me. Luckily, Floody stepped in, not with arms flailing to sort out the Welsh guys but with a comment that took all the heat out of the situation, by pushing me away and saying: 'Leave him, he's special.' Thanks, Floody – I think!

We built on that lead really well and, early in the second half, my second match in the Six Nations got a lot better with my second try.

It was unusual in one respect, because it was created when Mark Cueto found me with a pass. It doesn't happen too often and weeks later he was still going on about it, saying I owed him. I tried to give him one back against France, but he was just too slow and couldn't get there in time!

Wales did come back into it towards the end, as we knew they would, because they're a quality team. They scored a try through Morgan Stoddart and finished only a converted try behind us.

I also incurred Johnno's wrath (so it was lucky I had already scored two tries) by giving away a stupid penalty in the second half. They had been putting us under a lot of pressure so instinctively I put my hand in a ruck and before I knew it the referee had blown and they had scored three points.

I looked nervously up at the big screen when I was jogging back and sure enough there was Johnno's face looking like thunder – he was going mad. After the game, he said: 'Don't be doing anything like that again.'

It was a clear penalty and as I was running back I was

getting it from all sides as Steve Thompson had a pop as well. 'Pack it in,' he barked at me. I thought, 'What's going on here – I've got my own team-mates having a go at me.'

We're at a level when it doesn't matter whether someone shouts at you or not. You know when you've done something wrong. Sometimes you have to be firm with people, especially at Test level as one silly error can cost the game. I know I shouldn't have done it but it was a lack of concentration as we had defended for such a long period of time. I felt we needed to get the ball back and tried too hard to make it happen.

Steve Thompson had come on as a sub in the second half, along with a couple of other World Cup winners in Jonny Wilkinson and Simon Shaw. Shawsy was pretty annoyed because he broke his nose within a few minutes of appearing. He does play in one of those stupid positions where you will break your nose but that wasn't helping Shawsy's humour, especially as I was laughing at him. He might not admit it but I think there's a bit of vanity there.

I was standing with Fodes when Jonny came on and with almost his first touch he kicked a very long penalty.

Ben and I have little random chats sometimes during a game. I said, 'What kind of team is it when you can bring Jonny Wilkinson off the bench and he can kick a penalty like that straightaway?'

The influence of those experienced players ensured we held on to win by seven points. Floody was quite rightly named Man of the Match – he put us round the park beautifully. We had a few turnovers so there could have been more chances. It was all down to the forwards at the end. They did the hard graft.

After the game Johnno was definitely more annoyed about the penalty I gave away than anything else and I was a bit naive when responding to the media, which led to Johnno having a word with me.

The reporters gathered around us for interviews as they always do and one of them asked whether I felt I was seven points up across the whole game because I had scored two tries (ten) and given away a penalty (three). I just shrugged and said, 'Yes, you're right, I suppose so.' And it was printed in the papers as if I had actually said it, which I hadn't – I'd only agreed with them. Johnno asked me whether I had said that and I explained what had happened, which seemed to satisfy him. It helped that we had won the game.

My dive in the act of scoring started to become a story on its own after this match. The media were asking me about it and I was replying, 'Did I do that?' I wasn't aware of what I did. I had no idea I'd done that.

I suppose it showed me how magnified something can be if you do it playing for England and in a game that millions of people are watching on TV. The media kept going on about it and I struggled at first to appreciate the significance of it. After this Test week it changed, however, as I started to buy into it more.

The day ended in quite a surreal way as Warren Gatland took the chance to apologise to Dylan for what he had said about him.

England v Australia, 13 November 2010: I was away, with almost the whole length of the Twickenham pitch ahead of me.

At the end of my 100-metre run, I dived high and handsome over the line . . .

. . . then I looked up to the heavens. I dedicated the try to my father.

Cuets, Fodes and Dyl were going crazy. If only I could put that feeling in a bottle it would be worth a lot of money.

England v New Zealand, 6 November 2010: There was no cheering me up when we lost to the All Blacks. 'Next time we play you,' I thought, 'I'll remember today and how it feels to be on the losing side.'

England v South Africa, 27 November 2010: After being knocked out early in the match, I had no idea where I was for most of the game.

England v Wales, 4 February 2011: To score the first try of the 2011 Six Nations was a pretty special moment in my career.

Winning in Cardiff was an important milestone but we kept our feet on the ground. Here I am celebrating the win with my Northampton team-mates Dyl, Woody and Fodes.

England v Italy, 12 February 2011: Not even I thought it was possible to score four tries in one Six Nations match for England. Here's the first . . .

The second . . .

The third . . .

. . . and the fourth. I did a huge dive – I looked up at the big screen on my way back and Johnno was laughing.

I knew scoring four tries was a big deal but I wasn't aware that no one had done it for England since 1914. To achieve something I had never considered possible was certainly weird.

England v France, 26 February 2011: I thought for one moment I had got my seventh try of the tournament but it was disallowed for a forward pass. That decision really frustrated me.

England v Scotland, 13 March 2011: We thought we would throw everything at Scotland, but I think we tensed up as a squad as the title came into view.

England v Ireland, 19 March 2011: Stuck out on the wing, this game was intensely frustrating for me. We started to fall behind and there was nothing I could do about it.

I look back on the Six Nations campaign with pride. Being presented with the trophy made us realise what we achieved. It was something tangible.

The 2010–11 Premiership season kicked off with a massive game: Leicester at home. And to top it all off we beat our biggest rivals 27–19.

We went to London Irish in April and I managed to score a try which was later confirmed as the Premiership try of the season.

We progressed to the Premiership semi-final against Leicester where I was hit not once, not twice, but three times by Manu Tuilagi. I was told I did well to stay on my feet.

The first Heineken Cup game against Cardiff Blues was pretty fiery in December. I scored, which was great as I had been away with England for a while so I wanted to repay the lads.

In the Heineken Cup semis Perpignan didn't seem to be the Perpignan we knew and had watched. We won 23–7.

One of our key goals that season was to get to the Heineken Cup final and we had made it. I'm celebrating here with Fodes and Paul Diggin.

We were very down after losing to Leinster in the final, but Northampton shouldn't see the 2010–11 season as a failure because we reached a Heineken Cup final and Aviva Premiership semi-final.

Wales

I was sitting next to Dyl at the after-match function and Gatland came over. He reached across me and apologised for what had been said. Dyl accepted it but was still annoyed that someone had picked him out as a weakness. He was happy that Gatland had come up to him, but the fact he had gone out and played really well, proving Gatland wrong on the pitch, made Dyl happier than any apology he might have got.

Dyl wasn't the only Northampton player to turn in a world-class performance and looking back on the game I was particularly pleased for Tom Wood. Many people thought it was foolish to give Woody his Test debut in a game of this magnitude but I never had any doubts and he turned in such a solid game. He got better as the game went on, after collecting himself in the early stages.

It was a satisfying way to start the Six Nations. After the win over Australia in the autumn people had started getting carried away but we aren't like that. We know where we are as a team. We took a step closer with the win against Wales, but we will always keep our feet on the ground.

It shouldn't be underestimated, though, in terms of the development of the team, that Cardiff is a very difficult place for England to win. It was an important milestone. For a lot of the younger lads who had never played here, it was a massive step forwards.

We went back to the hotel for some food and although the head was up for a big night out in Cardiff, even though it was midnight, the body turned me down, so I had to plump for an early night. My lovely bed was calling.

Wales 19 England 26

Wales
Try: Stoddart. **Con:** S Jones. **Pens:** S Jones 3, Hook
J Hook; M Stoddart, J Davies, J Roberts, S Williams;
S Jones, M Phillips; P James, M Rees (capt), C Mitchell,
AW Jones, B Davies, D Lydiate, S Warburton, A Powell
Replacements: L Byrne for S Jones (67), D Peel for Phillips
(69), R Hibbard for Rees (70), J Yapp for Mitchell (71),
J Thomas for Lydiate (71), R Jones for Powell (33)
Sin-bin: Mitchell (46)

England
Tries: Ashton 2. **Cons:** Flood 2 **Pens:** Flood 3, Wilkinson
B Foden; C Ashton, M Tindall (capt), S Hape, M Cueto;
T Flood, B Youngs; A Sheridan, D Hartley, D Cole,
L Deacon, T Palmer, T Wood, J Haskell, N Easter
Replacements: J Wilkinson for Flood (66), D Care for Youngs
(62), D Wilson for Sheridan (61), S Thompson for Hartley
(69), S Shaw for Deacon (69), J Worsley for Haskell (62)
Sin-bin: Deacon (28)

Attendance: 74,276
Referee: A Rolland (Ireland)

5

Splashdown – Italy, France and Scotland

Scoring one try at Twickenham is a dream come true, scoring two or three is ridiculous, but to score four? Well, not even I, with my vivid imagination, thought it was possible to score four tries in one Six Nations Test match for England. But that's exactly what happened to me against Italy in our second game of the championship in 2011.

Prior to the game, scoring a try hadn't even crossed my mind, even though I had scored twice against Wales the weekend before. All I was focused on was helping England to another victory.

As it transpired, the game couldn't really have gone any better. Just like against Wales, Floody was through a gap before I knew it and we were on our way to the try-line. Try time!

I had around 40 metres to run in and I remember thinking, 'This is it. Do I dive or don't I?' And when I got close to the line I thought, 'Bugger it, just do it.' And that's exactly what I did.

The fuss about my swallow dive had been growing all week, and little did I know during the build-up that the Italy game would be the day when things started to go a bit nuts. But I honestly hadn't rehearsed or thought about the dive for this game.

It had, in fact, reached annoying proportions. It seemed everyone else was talking about it.

In fact, so many people had had their say about it that it's a wonder I didn't run over the dead-ball line as I considered all my options!

This time, though, my dive almost had big repercussions as it had clearly annoyed one of the Italian players, Gonzalo Canale. As I was getting to my feet, he came charging up to me intent on dishing something out.

Luckily Floody was there again, picking up the ball for the conversion, and he got in between us just as Canale was looking like he was about to lose the plot. You know you're struggling when Floody is doing your fighting. Similar to what happened against Wales, Floody defused the situation by saying: 'Leave him alone, he's an idiot!'

When I got up, I was smiling and laughing about it, wondering why Canale was letting my dive bother him. Why couldn't he just get on with his game? He was tugging and pulling me but I wasn't bothered and Floody just pushed him out of the way, picked up his ball and went to take the kick.

The dive had almost taken over the week running up to the game. I just wanted people to shut up about it, but I still couldn't stop myself doing it. For some reason I thought the thing to shut them up was to do it, but of course it only made the dive an even bigger story.

I know the dive looks more dangerous than it seems to me and, as I said before, it's true that I did once get the ball knocked out of my hand as I dived over the line, against Edinburgh in the Heineken Cup. But I haven't dropped the ball in the process of scoring and I hope I never will.

When I scored my long-range try against Australia the previous autumn, I dived then as well, but no one seemed to notice. Or if they did, it provoked little comment. Against Australia I did a dive with one hand up, with the ball safely tucked under the other arm. What seems to worry people is when I have the ball up high, in the hand that's raised to the sky, as I dive.

However, the simple truth is that I hadn't rehearsed it, I hadn't planned it, and the only thing in my mind during the Six Nations was trying to help England win a rugby match.

I'm told that in the first World Cup in 1987, Zimbabwe centre Richard Tsimba had a trademark try celebration that was a little bit similar to mine. He would launch himself skyward, holding the ball in both hands, and touch it down before landing on his head and completing a forward roll. When he scored his second try against Romania, he landed on his shoulder and dislocated it, ending his part in the match.

England's attack coach, Brian Smith, highlighted his concern when he showed the whole team the famous Juan Manuel Leguizamón incident. When Juan was playing for London Irish, he dived in the act of scoring and embarrassingly dropped the ball – it was even in front of the Sky TV cameras.

No one had mentioned anything to me but at the end of our video session preparing for the Italy match, Brian just put the footage on and said: 'This is how not to score tries.' And then he showed my try against Wales, adding: 'Lads, let's just make sure we score our tries properly.'

I think he was being serious because Smithy is quite a serious bloke, and he likes to know that you've listened to what he has said. He didn't do that one-on-one with me because he wanted to make sure everyone knew his view. That's how he works. We had a bit of a joke about it in the squad and we all laughed.

Other England players were doing the dive in training and videoing themselves doing it, so it was certainly spreading. I even received a letter from a man whose lad had dived in training and had broken his arm. It was all becoming a bit of a sideshow and I was starting to fear it was distracting from everything else that the team wanted to achieve.

After the opening Six Nations game against Wales, people started asking me about it but I wasn't taking too much notice. But in the run-up to our first home game against Italy, I started buying into it myself. I did a media session before the Italy game and all anyone wanted to ask me about was the dive. No one seemed to care about the two tries I scored against Wales – every question was about the dive and whether Martin Johnson or Brian Smith had given me an ultimatum about it.

We were still at Pennyhill Park – you don't come into contact with too many people there as it's head down for training – so the only way I could gauge the impact was with the media. And yes, I had far more media requests than ever before. Everyone wanted to know if I was going to do it again but I didn't really know – I had no idea what I was going to do if I scored against Italy. Luckily, I got the chance to find out.

I was surprised by the fuss. I'm not the only one to do it, but the change took place in the match against Wales, where I had held the ball out in front. Members of the public were coming up to me and saying: 'Don't drop that ball!'

A lot of the build-up to the Italy game centred round whether Johnno had spoken to me about it, what had he said to me and whether I would do it again. But Johnno had never said a word to me.

Like I say, the truth was I didn't know myself until the opportunity came around.

Splashdown

Taking on Italy was a little like playing Samoa three months earlier. We were coming into the game off the back of a big win and they were the dangerous outsiders. People know Italy aren't the sort of side that can win a World Cup but you can't treat them lightly. They're improving every year and had almost beaten Ireland on the opening weekend of the tournament.

This was also going to be my first home game in the Six Nations, so I was hardly going to ease up. I need to play well in every game, but that was especially the case this time.

Amazingly, soon after my first try I scored again. This time it was a move we'd planned in the week, with Shontayne Hape making the room for me and me appearing on his shoulder. Two former rugby league lads working in unison.

We knew Shontayne would have a good chance of getting through the gap, as he spun to make the offload, so all I had to do was follow on his inside and take the pass.

Nine times out of ten, moves we plan in the run-up to a game never work so when they come off it's time for an even bigger celebration. For once all the hard work was worth it.

No one mentioned the dive at half-time and even though I had scored twice, the biggest celebration came for Mark Cueto's try. Cuets is one of the most popular players in the squad and remarkably for a winger he hadn't scored in his previous eighteen Tests, so when he got over you could see the joy on everyone's faces. People were genuinely happy for him.

I was certainly caning him over his barren run (in a jokey way!) but there's no doubt he was playing really well, perhaps some of his best rugby for England. He was playing as well as I was but not scoring.

Sometimes it was a source of banter among the team. You could see it irritated him so we'd chuck it in there and I think it shows we're good mates when you can be relaxed with each other. He takes it well but it was a huge relief for him when he did finally score and you could see the other players felt that too with the way they were running over and congratulating him.

We led 31–6 at the break so it was a pretty contented dressing room. No one was taking the win for granted but it's a lot easier to do those half-times than it is when we're losing. And when we did come out for the second half we carried on in almost exactly the same way.

It went from good to brilliant for me as I scored my first 'pick and go' try to bring up my hat-trick, going in from only a couple of yards out, just like a forward would. Banners (Matt Banahan) crashed through and I was screaming my head off but he didn't look like he had any intention of passing, because his eyes were set on the line. As soon as he got tackled, Nick Easter came in and was trying to nudge me out of the way. But I was having none of it and I grabbed the ball and dived over. When a game opens up like that it seems that everyone thinks they can start scoring tries. It's strange but it always happens.

Splashdown

A hat-trick is amazing enough but soon afterwards there followed my fourth. I can hardly believe I'm saying *my fourth* – my fourth try in a Test match. This wasn't supposed to happen. One is the norm, if you're lucky, but no one scores four tries in a championship match – well, no one (I found out later) for England since Ronnie Poulton-Palmer in 1914.

And again it was a Banners assist. He stormed through and we only had one man to beat when he slipped it to me. I had another 40 metres to run and obviously did a huge dive, the big difference being that when I looked up at the big screen on my way back Johnno was laughing. I suppose you would if your wing has just scored his fourth try and your team is top of the Six Nations table.

He saw the joke in it, which probably doesn't happen too often. And that carried on into the dressing room after the game.

Afterwards, I was hauled in front of the TV cameras as the Man of the Match, so I was the only one not in the changing rooms celebrating what turned out to be a stunning win. Johnno told the players: 'Chris is out there doing his last-ever interview as an England player,' referring to my dive! Once I was told about that I knew things were okay.

I'm glad that he and the coaches saw the funny side of it and didn't dwell on the fact that I shouldn't have been doing it. I think Johnno is okay about it . . . just as long as I don't drop the ball.

I knew scoring four tries was a big deal but I wasn't aware of the full significance, of the fact that no Englishman had done it in the championship since Poulton-Palmer, the England captain, against France in Paris on 13 April 1914. The final International played before World War I. To achieve something I had never considered possible was certainly weird.

I also equalled the record for tries in one Six Nations as I had now scored six, so the records just kept coming. As you can imagine, my media demands went through the roof and after a little bit of celebrating I went to answer a barrage of questions, with print, radio and TV media all interviewing me.

The other players, who told me what Johnno had said, were taking the mickey out of me as they felt I hadn't listened and was still diving. The typical comment was that I was going to be dropped because of the dive. They were their same old selves, which is a good thing and what you want. I don't want anything to change, especially when I'm scoring tries. Scoring tries is something I love doing and something I want to carry on doing for as long as I can.

When I got to the post-match dinner, young lads were throwing themselves on the floor in front of me, kids of people going to dinner. I was just standing there with friends and family and there were these kids diving in front of me, like I had dived in the game. Nothing like that had happened before and I realised it had really caught on.

Suddenly everyone wanted to know about my dive. Some christened it the Ash Splash. People wanted to know whether I had been practising it with Ben Foden, or whether I had made it up on the spur of the moment. Had we been rehearsing the move? Had Martin Johnson authorised it? I started to realise celebrations like this were very unusual in rugby union. All people wanted to talk to me about was the dive, not the win or the fact I'd scored four tries.

In the dinner I seemed to have gained a new-found fame as people came up to talk to me. It wasn't anything like the attention Jonny Wilkinson gets, but it certainly made me feel odd. This was very different even from the Australia try or the two against Wales the week before. The attention wasn't something I wanted or sought but it didn't make me feel uncomfortable as I knew it was part of success. I kind of embraced it, but the way I've been brought up I'm not the sort of person to get carried away with it.

Alex Corbisiero, the American-born prop, had made his England debut in the game as a late replacement for Andrew Sheridan, who had picked up an injury in training.

It's crucial that players can come in without breaking stride and Alex, who had been in and around the squad for just a short while, did just that. I was impressed by the way he came in on the Thursday and played as if he had been in the squad for years. Being without Sheridan for a game like that, when there was a big focus on the scrum, was a big loss. But Alex conducted himself superbly and was clearly the right man for the job. He has an Italian-American family so it made it an even bigger game for him.

That week, as there wasn't a bus journey for us, we made

Alex do his song for the team – which every new cap does – in front of us all in the dressing room.

I didn't know him that well but it became clear he was a bit of a rap fan. He's quite the rapper, but he did make the mistake of stopping when people started throwing things at him. The key thing is to carry on! He didn't know you were meant to carry on regardless so he made it ten times worse. Eventually he got going again and finished it.

After listening to Alex, the texts were flying in. It's the same whenever we win. About sixty were waiting for me when I turned on my phone – it's a very different story when we lose!

More than anything, my mum was worried about what Johnno would say about the dive. She said: 'Did he have a go at you about the dive?' To which I answered no, even though I knew that deep down it did bother him. Of course she was delighted but she's my mum so she's always going to be more worried about what the coaches have said, rather than the tries I've scored.

My mum also made sure she came to the black-tie dinner, because she thought I was going to get an award for scoring four tries. Of course that didn't happen, although I did have my Man of the Match trophy with me.

The Australia try was something that I had always dreamed of doing but scoring four tries in one game for England wasn't in my wildest dreams. How could it have been?

No one ever thinks they will score four tries in a match, let alone in a Six Nations match for England.

Splashdown

Back at the team hotel a lot of the players headed out for a few celebratory beers, but I was drained by the day's events so decided to head for the safety of the hotel bar, with Melissa, and the comfort of a steak sandwich and chips with Dyl and his girlfriend, Tins and Zara, and a few other players. Glorious!

I felt more comfortable going back and spending time with the people closest to me, rather than heading into central London and cracking open the champagne. I wanted to have a chance to sit back calmly and reflect on what had happened that day, rather than heading off for a big night out. We had been in camps for four weeks by the time of the Italy game so that probably aided my desire to chill out, before we grabbed a well-earned week off in advance of France coming to Twickenham.

It's odd sometimes to think that one of your team-mates is in a relationship with a woman who's thirteenth in line to the throne, a bona fide member of the royal family. Zara is a really lovely girl and has absolutely no airs and graces.

After one of the games in the autumn, Prince Harry came into the dressing room and when he headed to the back of the changing room to speak to Tins I went after him to say hello and shake his hand, because it's not every day you get to meet a prince. It was only a few seconds later that I realised I had done it completely naked! Well, I was on the way to the shower, although I'm not sure what he must have thought. I just wanted to take my chance to say hello. I don't think he thought anything of it.

England 59 Italy 13

England
Tries: Ashton 4, Cueto, Tindall, Care, Haskell **Cons:** Flood 5, Wilkinson 3 **Pen:** Flood

B Foden; C Ashton, M Tindall (capt), S Hape, M Cueto; T Flood, B Youngs; A Corbisiero, D Hartley, D Cole, L Deacon, T Palmer, T Wood, J Haskell, N Easter

Replacements: M Banahan for Cueto (50), J Wilkinson for Flood (55), D Care for Youngs (55), S Thompson for Hartley (50), D Wilson for Cole (62), S Shaw for Deacon (46), H Fourie for Wood (62)

Italy
Try: Ongaro **Con:** Bergamasco **Pens:** Bergamasco 2

L McLean; A Masi, G Canale, A Sgarbi, Mi Bergamasco; L Orquera, F Semenzato; S Perugini, L Ghiraldini, M Castrogiovanni, C Del Fava, Q Geldenhuys, V Bernabo, A Zanni, S Parisse (capt)

Replacements: K Burton for McLean (79), G Garcia for Sgarbi (59), F Ongaro for Ghiraldini (66), A Lo Cicero (56) and S Perugini (63) for Castrogiovanni, S Dellape for Del Fava (47), R Barbieri for Bernabo (60)

Sin-bin: Castrogiovanni (44)

Attendance: 80,810
Referee: C Joubert (South Africa)

Splashdown

There was a lot of pressure in the camp in the week before we played France. This was considered the main game for us, the game that would decide if we were going to be European champions for the first time since 2003. Yet we didn't see it that way. We simply saw it as the next game and a match in which we just wanted to carry on playing well.

I felt that as France were such a good side it was also our chance to prove a point, to prove we were actually going somewhere as a team, starting to play together and produce good rugby. It was an opportunity to show we could play against France as we had done against Italy, so it was a pretty tense week.

Talk of a Grand Slam was irrelevant at this point. It genuinely wasn't spoken about within the squad as we all knew we'd only won two games at this point, so why take up energy speaking or even thinking about a Grand Slam?

The team selected was more or less the one that had lost to France in Paris almost a year earlier, so a focus of the week was our belief that we hadn't done ourselves justice in that game and that we wanted to put that right, publicly. We had played really well in Paris and came very close but we hadn't got the victory we desired.

Another national coach, this time France's Marc Lièvremont, decided to try to get under our skin by telling anyone who would listen that no one likes the English.

Four weeks after Warren Gatland had tried to undermine Dylan Hartley, here was Lièvremont stirring things up. I don't know why people do that as all it does is spur on those you're trying to get at. It made us want to play even better against France. He was having a go at the whole nation, rather than a player in the team like Gatland had done, but we still used his words in our build-up to the game, and Johnno told us to use it.

This match was a great opportunity to see exactly where we were in the championship, especially as we were at home again. I felt we needed to start making a point of playing at home, start building a 'fortress' where no team expected to win.

England teams before us had built up long winning runs at Twickenham and used that as a basis to go on and win Grand Slams and World Cups, and that was our aim too.

Nerves were starting to build after two wins, and that could have been significant in what turned out to be a less than flowing performance. Those nerves started to get greater and greater as the tournament went on. England hadn't been in that position for a while and moving forward it's something we're going to have to learn to cope with better.

We're such a young team and looking back it's easy to see we started to cramp up a bit as the tournament went on, something that affected our performances. At the time you don't see it creeping up, but it was clearly in the back of our minds.

Nonetheless, we mustn't be too hard on ourselves as we did still beat France, something not every recent England team has done. Nor did the weather help us at Twickenham that day.

We wanted to play wide, but it was difficult. We still believed we could go out there and do what we wanted against France, but the expectation was such that I felt we could almost touch it.

This was a match we had to win, rather than a match we wanted to win, which was a crucial change in attitude. It was a new mindset, not just for the players, but for the supporters and almost anyone connected with English rugby. It wasn't a conscious change, it wasn't something we wanted to happen, but it was still there and the feeling only built as the tournament went on.

I thought we dealt with the expectation well, despite the bad weather, and that we beat France well. Maybe we didn't play as well as we wanted to, with a lot of mistakes creeping in. But that's going to happen in a new team. Crucially, we did what we needed to do and that was chalk up our third successive victory.

I didn't get on the score sheet but Fodes (Ben Foden) did, even though I know I should have got there before him. Fodes never seems to get the number of tries his performances deserve, whether for Northampton or England, so it was great to see him get over the line against the French.

This was the day that Jonny Wilkinson came on to seal the game. Even if you aren't looking at the bench you know when Jonny is coming on as the crowd go absolutely nuts every time he takes to the field.

Typically of Jonny, he was saying afterwards that the ovation was also for Floody going off, but you only had to be on the pitch to see the truth. It doesn't bother Toby. He's not the sort of guy to let it bother him.

It doesn't matter who you are, or what country you're in, as soon as Jonny steps on the pitch the crowd go mad. When I first came into the team I was in complete awe of Jonny. I remember the day after one game I was having physio in a room overlooking the gym at Pennyhill Park and there was Jonny flogging himself on this rowing machine. He wasn't just going through the session in a half-hearted way – he was nailing it. And this was the day after a game, when we're meant to be taking it easier.

I don't think I've ever seen anyone work as hard as that guy.

Whenever we finish a training session and we're knackered on the side of the pitch, he does more fitness. He stays out longer, and works as hard as he possibly can. It's no wonder the guy has achieved what he has.

I don't know how he does it but the other lads say he's been that way since he was eighteen. I'm in awe of him because of his attitude and because of his record. I've never seen anything like his work ethic and probably never will.

If he'd stayed fit he'd have more than 120 caps now and along the way he has often been the world's record point-scorer – he's now vying with Dan Carter – and seems to have broken every other record on offer. Penalties, drop-goals, conversions – you name it, Jonny has the record.

But someone would have to have more than a shed-load of points or tries to their name for me to be in awe of them. True respect comes from the way a player conducts himself on and off the pitch. Jonny is exemplary, the ultimate team man, who always (and I mean always) puts the team first.

He's non-stop. We'll do fitness, everyone will go in and have their shower and some food – and Jonny just carries on with his kicking. I'm just delighted I was able to start my England career alongside him and that he's in my team and not on the other side.

I also get on well with him, as Jonny gets on with everyone. What's not to like?

He's not as quiet as everyone thinks he is, though. You couldn't be if you're an outside-half because you need to bark the orders and lay down the law when the time comes.

His ability was probably summed up ahead of the France game. In one of the training sessions, when the starting team were on one side against everyone else, Jonny was on the opposing side as he was on the bench and we were running some moves. He got the ball on the twenty-two and went to kick it. I thought I had it covered as I was standing in position, exactly where I was meant to be. But Jonny had other ideas.

He kicked with his right foot across field and landed it about two inches inside the touchline, where it bounced up perfectly for Delon Armitage to run in for a try. We all stopped and were saying: 'Jonny, what did you do that for?!' He made us all look pretty stupid! I asked him how on earth he had done that and he just shrugged his shoulders, again refusing to take any praise for what was an awesome piece of skill – one of the best I've seen on a rugby pitch. He nonchalantly jogged back as if it was something he did every day of the week.

And when he ran on in the match with France he responded to the crowd's reaction by closing the game out for us superbly. He was just what we needed at the time, and it's only because Floody was playing so well that Jonny couldn't get into the starting line-up in the Six Nations.

He must have been frustrated with the way it was in the championship, but I also know he was aware of and appreciated how well Floody was playing, and I think in a way he enjoyed his new role off the bench. He also knows he needs to help Floody's development. Jonny would never accept being on the bench all the time but he understood the new role he was filling at the start of 2011, which involved a big leadership role in the side.

The feeling in the squad before the France game was excellent. There's a great mix of youth, and then you have experienced campaigners like Cueto and Tindall.

We all get on really well, both as players and as mates, and that really helps us.

It's brilliant to have people like Cuets and Tins around. They've been there many times before and help me immeasurably in terms of positional play and defence.

But I'm not hiding and if I've something to say I'll say it. It cuts both ways and we're all humble enough to learn from each other.

We're getting to know each other almost like a club side now and that's great. Saying that, I'd like a little more time to work on defence, fielding box kicks and the like, but that will come and every moment spent together is a moment well spent.

I went into the France game with six tries in the championship, the equal highest tally for one Six Nations tournament, and I thought for one moment I had got my seventh when I ran in, but it was disallowed for a forward pass.

There was another chance that I didn't make the most of and I just didn't do as well as I'd hoped, but I still can't work out what was wrong with my try in the French match. I was called back for a pass which I'm sure wasn't forward. They penalise forward passes like that in league, but I've never seen it in union. Maybe they're making an example of me – every time they see me running up the middle of the pitch now they're going to blow the whistle for a forward pass, because they don't want to see that dive!

That decision really frustrated me. I didn't think about it before or during the game but afterwards I was thinking about the record a little bit, as so many people mentioned it to me. I tried not to dwell on it but it was impossible because so many people were going on about the record.

It goes back to what Paul Grayson says to me at Northampton: my game always drops off when I think about scoring tries, or even go looking for them. I have to play my game and they will come, but I find that harder the more tries I score.

We were delighted with the way we won but disappointed with the way we had played, I think because it had gone so well against Wales and Italy. We wanted to play better, especially as we were at home, and in the aftermath of the match I was trying to remind myself this was France, one of the best teams in the world. We will always be happy with beating a side like France, who arrived as the reigning Grand Slam champions. However, the level of unhappiness in the dressing room after the game showed me that the side was setting itself newer and higher standards – which is a good thing.

We weren't depressed but it was annoying for the game to go that way.

England 17 France 9

England
Try: Foden **Pens:** Flood 3, Wilkinson
B Foden; C Ashton, M Tindall (capt), S Hape, M Cueto;
T Flood, B Youngs; A Sheridan, D Hartley, D Cole,
L Deacon, T Palmer, T Wood, J Haskell, N Easter
Replacements: M Banahan for Hape (76), J Wilkinson for Flood (51), D Care for Youngs (63), A Corbisiero for Sheridan (23), S Thompson for Hartley (67), H Fourie for Cole (76), S Shaw for Deacon (71)

Splashdown

France

Pens: Yachvili 3

C Poitrenaud; Y Huget, A Rougerie, Y Jauzion, V Clerc;
F Trinh-Duc, D Yachvili; T Domingo, W Servat, N Mas,
J Pierre, L Nallet, T Dusautoir (capt), I Harinordoquy,
S Chabal

Replacements: D Traille for Poitrenaud (51), A Palisson for
Trinh-Duc (67), M Parra for Yachvili (62), S Marconnet for
Domingo (60), G Guirado for Servat (76), J Thion for
Pierre (62), J Bonnaire for Chabal (51)

Attendance: 82,107

Referee: G Clancy (Ireland)

The France game was followed by a week off. I say we were given a week off, but it wasn't like we were going on holiday. It was a week off from having a match but the England squad was still together and Johnno made a good decision to break from our normal base in Bagshot and move the squad to Oxford. The change was as good as a rest, although when we got back into training on the Tuesday it was just as intense. We got the chance to have a few nights out as a squad, which was great because with the intensity of the first two weeks, and everything appearing to go at 100mph, it's easy to forget the benefit of a few beers together.

Every place we seemed to go that week was chaos. From being largely anonymous in many of the places I might go out, we were recognised almost everywhere we went in Oxford. On the first night a few of us went out for a quiet beer, but we literally couldn't get away from our table. I was there with Danny (Care), Shontayne (Hape), Fodes and Nick (Easter). We had a long table in this one bar and it ended with around 100 people crowding round us at one point. I hadn't experienced anything like it, and wouldn't want to experience it on too many nights out again. Just four or five of us going out turned into something quite ridiculous. I like a night out with friends but that was a difficult night.

The management trust us to do our own thing in these 'off' weeks, but we all had the Scotland game in the back of our minds. We might have a few beers but as long as you're there for training the next day the management won't mind. It was a chance to let our hair down. I wouldn't eat what I really wanted as I was trying to eat healthily, even though I had a few drinks.

After Oxford we had the weekend off and I decided to shoot back up to Wigan to see my family because chances like that don't come round too often. But on that weekend I found being recognised a bit tough. Things had changed in Wigan as well. My face had been in the papers and on TV an awful lot more in the weeks beforehand and it got me some unwanted attention when I was back in Wigan.

People were asking for pictures – which isn't a problem – when they would never have asked before. Before playing for England, I had been just a local lad who played for Wigan.

Although I was used to people asking for pictures, things seemed to have changed this time and the people involved weren't necessarily rugby fans. Some of the comments had an edge to them, an edge I didn't like.

I'll stop and chat to anyone but I was aware of guys trying to wind me up or pick a fight, when they would never have done so before. I seemed to be more of a target than ever, especially when I got split up from my friends.

I was glad to be around the lads I had known since I was a child. Obviously they were no different, treating me just as they always have. I started to worry a little more about people stitching me up, as they might with footballers, and I was beginning to attract the sort of person who wanted to cause trouble.

I don't know if it was jealousy or not, young lads trying to cause trouble. You might be in a place where you think you know everyone and suddenly you're on your own. At one point a while ago I might have got myself into trouble and got away with it, but there comes a time when you realise you can't be like that any more. I realised incidents off the field could affect my chances of going to a World Cup, and it just isn't worth it. I suddenly realised I was in places where a lot of people know who you are, so your behaviour has to be spot on.

I also took the chance to go to a Salford v Wigan friendly game. There were a few shouts from the crowd, like: 'Does this mean you're coming back?' or 'What are you doing here?' I get a lot of stick about having become too posh when I go back. I have to sit with my brother for a good hour and have a conversation with him before I go anywhere, otherwise I get a load of abuse for my accent. Everyone there thinks that anyone outside of Wigan is a Cockney!

Despite this it was a very welcome few days off and I got to see family and friends, before returning to England for the Scotland Test week.

The week off hadn't changed the level of pressure and if anything, with three wins under our belt, it intensified, especially as we all knew how desperate Scotland would be to derail our title challenge.

The Scots hadn't had a good championship and there was a lot of talk about how they couldn't win at Twickenham, which is just what we didn't want to hear! Scotland are dangerous enough as it is without everyone writing them off as well. Those days always end up hard and that turned out to be the case in the Scotland match.

Their finishing position in recent Six Nations championships is the reason they're written off, but their recent record against England is excellent, and so it proved again.

In the lead-up to the match even my Northampton teammate Joe Ansbro – who had just made his debut for Scotland – got on the diving bandwagon by saying they were going to make sure I didn't have a chance to do it again.

In the press before the match it might have sounded like I was annoyed but it was part of a long-running joke between me and Joe. Even Tom Wood got involved, saying in an interview that I had copied the dive off Paul Diggin, another Northampton player.

Joe knew what he said would get to me – and it did, but not in a bad way. Joe is a good player and did very well for Northampton. But his chances at Franklin's Gardens were limited because he had Jon Clarke in front of him and that's one of the reasons Joe decided to join London Irish. He's a solid player who has been performing well for Scotland.

At the time there was no sense of us trying to get back on track following a disappointing performance against France but, looking back, the atmosphere in the squad wasn't as good as it could have been.

Once you join up with the England squad you're in your little bubble and outside influences rarely get in. We thought we would put everything right against Scotland, but I think we tensed up as a squad as the title came into view. Teams overachieve when they play England and we have to get used to that. Every time someone plays at Twickenham it's their big day out, their big chance to put any problems behind them, and we need to recognise that. So Scotland's form going into this game was irrelevant.

I experienced some success with Wigan, but nothing prepares you for the sense of expectation that comes with playing for England at union. But don't get me wrong – I'm exactly where I want to be, achieving things with England.

At that time we were in the bubble, with everyone still

thinking we're going okay, that we're at home again, and so our only focus was to put right what we'd done wrong against France.

However, when the game started it was clear that all Scotland wanted to do was ruin how we play – and fair play to them, they did a great job of that. We wanted quick ball and wanted to be able to move it. Scotland set about stopping that. Despite that, we did get a lot of chances to score. We had a lot of breaks and each time we managed to mess it up, which made it an incredibly frustrating afternoon for us. Their game plan worked perfectly and they managed to put the right people in the right places to disrupt what we were trying to do. That's part of the process – we have to learn from these matches.

The victory made it four consecutive wins for us, and we should have been happy, but judging from the mood afterwards you would have thought we had lost. Looking around the dressing room it was clear that just winning wasn't good enough for this team, which is a good thing.

We didn't prove what we wanted to prove and we didn't play the way we wanted to play, so that's always going to be frustrating. Just winning is never good enough for England, never good enough for the fans and never good enough for the media. It's a combination that brings real pressure for the players.

For the younger lads like me, Fodes and Ben Youngs, this feeling is all new and it takes time to adjust to the level of expectation and the fact you're in the spotlight for every minute of every game.

We scored a good try through Tom Croft, the Leicester man coming off the bench and galloping down the left wing, but when he dived over I remember thinking that could have been my try. At the ruck I could see something was developing and part of me wanted to try to get on the end of the move, but something held me back! That's what happens to me when I start thinking about scoring tries and not enough about playing the way I normally play.

After the game we mixed well with the Scotland lads although I did have a run-in during the game with their hooker Scott Lawson, who plays at Gloucester. As we were running in at half-time I was annoyed because I hadn't seen much ball. Lawson, one of the replacements, was standing there at the side of the tunnel and said something to me like 'Were you out there?' I can't repeat what I said to him but it contained at least one expletive! It's not unusual to have exchanges like that as teams run in at half-time and he was clearly trying to annoy me.

I got my own back, though. When Crofty scored I made a point of running over to Lawson and tapping him around the back of the head as I went over to celebrate in the corner. I wish I'd have scored as I'd have gone and given him the ball.

The Scots were keen on upsetting us right from the start. At every ruck they were keen for a fight, but that's what happens when you have nothing to lose. The reality is that England have so much to lose, whenever and whoever they play. Before I started playing for the England team I didn't take any notice of the pressure they're put under or what comes with playing for them, but once you pull on the jersey it becomes unavoidable.

Against Scotland I still thought we played better than England had in previous years, so it certainly wasn't all doom and gloom. I didn't think the criticism that came our way after the Scotland game was justified, even if we didn't play as well as we were capable of.

Even though we were winning, with hindsight I can now see that we were getting more tense as a team in that build-up to Grand Slam week. After the match the coaches were talking about how well we'd done the job, but the focus turned immediately to the Grand Slam game in Ireland.

I went straight back home afterwards frustrated that we hadn't fulfilled our potential. I didn't even go via the hotel. I felt just as I had following the New Zealand game – as if we had lost.

However, there was no time for anything else as the Scotland game had taken place on a Sunday so Ireland was only six days away.

England 22 Scotland 16

England
Try: Croft **Con:** Wilkinson **Pens:** Flood 4, Wilkinson
B Foden; C Ashton, M Tindall (capt), S Hape, M Cueto;

Splashdown

T Flood, B Youngs; A Corbisiero, D Hartley, D Cole,
L Deacon, T Palmer, T Wood, J Haskell, N Easter
Replacements: M Banahan for Tindall (41), J Wilkinson for
Flood (66), D Care for Youngs (55), S Thompson for
Hartley (66), P Doran-Jones for Cole (75), S Shaw for
Deacon (66), T Croft for Wood (66)

Scotland
Try: Evans **Con:** Paterson **Pens:** Paterson 2 **Drop-goal:** Jackson
C Paterson; S Danielli, J Ansbro, S Lamont, M Evans;
R Jackson, R Lawson; A Jacobsen, R Ford, M Low, R Gray,
A Kellock (capt), N Hines, J Barclay, K Brown
Replacements: D Parks for Jackson (55), M Blair for Lawson
(55), S Lawson for Ford (66), G Cross for Low (53),
A Strokosch for Hines (68), R Vernon for Brown (43)
Sin-bin: Barclay (57)

Attendance: 82,120
Referee: R Poite (France) replaced by J Garces (France) (59)

6

The Grand Slam Dream Crushed

The moment we touched down at Dublin airport, you could sense the tension. The city is sports-mad and Dubliners love their rugby. Everyone has a word to say and an opinion to give, and from the off I started to appreciate how difficult it was going to be to defeat Ireland and claim England's first Six Nations Grand Slam in eight years.

I sensed that the nation was against us even more than it had been in Wales, and they're passionate enough!

Everywhere in Dublin you can feel something different. The day before the game a few of us were walking down the street and a couple of young Irish lads came up to welcome us to Dublin and wish us the best. But when they were a few yards past us they started giving us the finger. A small incident, sure, but it made me acutely aware of the passion of their supporters – it really felt like we were taking on the nation.

On that same day, one of the lads from Northampton, Jimmy (James) Downey, who is from Dublin, came to meet me and Dyl [Hartley] and we headed off to Wagamama's. The three of us were sitting there and before we knew it almost all the Leinster players in the Ireland team, including Brian O'Driscoll, Jonathan Sexton and Jamie Heaslip, came in as well and sat directly behind us.

Jimmy knows them but Brian was shaking his head at him sitting with us and wouldn't speak to him. Jimmy said O'Driscoll wasn't best pleased to see him there. Dyl and I weren't bothered, but it was a bit tense and after a while we left because we could feel their eyes burning into our backs.

We were still confident, though, because we'd arrived at the Aviva Stadium with four wins under our belts in the championship. We would have liked to have played better in the two previous games, against France and Scotland, but we still believed it was going to be our day. Sadly, in the event, we were wrong . . .

We also had a significant absentee to deal with: Mike Tindall had an injury and was a huge loss. Nick Easter came in and did a great job as skipper, but he was effectively our third-choice captain, as we knew Lewis Moody would have been captain had he been fit.

Mike is one of those players who, bizarrely in my view, doesn't get the praise outside of the squad he deserves. There are unsung heroes in every team and Tins is certainly ours – a player who does his job quietly but very well.

People see his defence and organisational skills, but in attack his abilities don't seem to be recognised. I think the criticism he gets is unfair. His worth to the team was demonstrated by how difficult it was to replace him in Dublin, and it will be just as difficult to replace him when he finally retires.

Tins is a big leader for the team, especially for backs like me. At the time you don't think anything of it. You think you'll be fine, and the attitude is 'we'll cope', but after the Ireland game I understood exactly how much we could have done with Tins on that day of all days. Like Johnno, he's been there, done that and printed the T-shirt.

But Matt Banahan had been playing very well, so no one had any doubts about his ability to come in. I don't know how Banners feels about it, but it was a big game to come into for your first ever start in the Six Nations, especially as most of his caps had been won on the wing. It was a big ask for him to play at 13, opposite O'Driscoll, but that's the way it goes sometimes.

I don't think Matt played badly – far from it – but he just got put out of the game completely and was unable to have the same impact he'd been having. I was slightly surprised by the Ireland selection, with Sexton starting at fly-half. I thought they would go with Ronan O'Gara. But as we discovered, they were a good combination, Sexton igniting their running game and O'Gara coming on late in the game to seal things up with his kicking game.

Before the match, defence coach Mike Ford had made a point of coming round and talking to me. In the autumn he'd told me that I'm at my best when I'm chilled out and relaxed. So before the Ireland match he asked how I was feeling. 'No problem, I'm fine,' I answered, but it was a pretence.

I wasn't okay. I just wanted to get on with it as I was going nuts with the waiting before that match. It was an evening kick-off to start with, so as usual the day really dragged and I couldn't relax. That just isn't how I am or how I want to play. I wanted to get on with it, and that is a bad sign for me.

Even the anthems and the presentation of the teams to the Irish president were killing me. I should have been able to enjoy the anthems as I do at Twickenham, but it shows how nervous I was and how the tension was building up.

It must have been building up for everyone and so it isn't surprising that it showed when the match started. The build-up is hard and I know it was difficult for everyone as there were so few players in the squad who had challenged for a Grand Slam. It certainly showed in the way we played.

Credit to Ireland, they did play well. They put us totally off our game, stopped us from doing almost anything we planned, and they defended like madmen. My mum always says the hungry fighter is the best fighter and Ireland had a lot of hungry fighters on the pitch that day.

Ireland hadn't been playing well, so this game was make or

break for them. Lose it and they would have finished the championship in fourth position with just two wins, and that in a World Cup year. So they had to win. At the time, of course, you don't think like that. You don't accept the desperation and motivation in other teams as it lessens your chances.

Ireland's backs were right against the wall and they played as if their lives depended on it. Their season would have been written off as a disaster if they had lost. Creating the hunger when you're on top and the favourites is something England's 2003 team mastered and it's something we must develop.

If they played like that against New Zealand, Ireland would win, no doubt in my mind, but it looked like it needed England coming to town, hunting a Grand Slam, to bring out that performance in them.

The game kicked off and they immediately put us in the corners. Added to this, the pressure meant we contributed to our own downfall by giving away too many penalties, and we lost Tom Palmer early on to injury. Looking back, did anything go right?

The frustration was getting to me and it boiled over a couple of times, leading me to have a couple of on-field clashes with the Ireland players, and in particular Sexton and O'Gara.

Early on I stupidly got involved in a running battle with Sexton. It was an indication of how wound up I was getting because when he was kicking I tried to put him off. The penalty was awarded against me for tackling him too high. So I tried to have a bit of a chat with him. I wanted to distract him by giving him abuse as he went to kick the penalty. I was saying 'Don't miss it' and 'You're rubbish', but when the ball sailed over he just laughed at me. It showed I was distracted and that my head wasn't right. Donncha O'Callaghan was waiting for me on the halfway line, and he gave me a load of stick as well.

When it went over I ended up laughing about it, but that's the way the game seemed to go from there. We lost Ben Youngs to the sin-bin after he threw the ball away to stop Ireland taking a quick lineout. I'm not sure if that was inexperience as well, a case of his head not being with it. We never really got a blow in; in fact, we never got anywhere near them in the eighty minutes.

We did score one try in the second half, when Steve Thompson, who'd come off the bench, sprinted in from 40 metres when he intercepted an Eoin Reddan pass at a lineout. But by then Ireland were effectively out of sight and the Grand Slam dream was gone.

Credit to Ireland, they played a real good game plan and taught us a big lesson, a big lesson about intensity and how it's so easy to get caught cold in a Test match.

Stuck out on the wing, it was intensely frustrating for me. We started to fall behind on the scoreboard and there was nothing I could do about it; Sexton hardly missed a kick all day.

In the second half I managed to have another confrontation – with O'Gara. He replaced Sexton and it looked as though I was carrying on my feud with Irishmen who play outside-half!

The Grand Slam Dream Crushed

I'd never met Ronan before. But I'd played against him twice and always seemed to find myself either on the floor with him or dragging him out of rucks.

He kicked a goal for Munster against Northampton and I ran out and gave him a load of abuse that day; he stopped and we had a bit of chat then! It has gone on from there.

This time he came on with about ten minutes remaining, and as soon as he appeared I could see him looking for me.

He was soon kicking all these banana kicks into the corner, pinning us back and reminding us there was simply no way back for us. My head went a little bit, due to the frustration of the situation, and as soon as we came near each other we were in for each other.

The first challenge was near the touchline with both of us grabbing the other. It was handbags stuff to be honest but everyone came in and I wouldn't let him go. Brian O'Driscoll was one of the first there and said: 'Come on, lads, pack it in, it's over . . . and so is the game!' And that just tipped me over the edge. A few minutes later when O'Gara got the ball again I flew out of the line to try to tackle him. My head was gone and we had lost the game and the Grand Slam!

I'm sure Ronan's not a fighter and neither am I, really.

I did manage to make one break during the game, deep into Ireland's twenty-two, but O'Driscoll used a bit of his experience to get the ball off me. As I was going to the floor and trying to offload, he called for the ball and as I didn't pick up the accent straightaway I passed it to him. Another lesson to learn!

Splashdown

At the end I was so disappointed that everything had gone wrong that I just knelt down and had a moment to myself. I thought about my dad and some of the conversations we'd had. I think about him all the time, but he was particularly in my thoughts then because we'd had a great chance to win something special and when you miss a chance like that it takes you back.

To his credit, O'Driscoll was very sympathetic to us in his post-match speech. He said it had taken him nine attempts to win a Grand Slam and that falling short is a valuable lesson. Brian spoke with a lot of honesty I thought. He explained that things didn't happen overnight and that it took Ireland a few years to get their Grand Slam, after coming so close. It takes time and experience to get to those places.

I appreciated what he said but all the time I was thinking that I hadn't come to Dublin to learn lessons – I had come to win a Grand Slam.

At the post-match dinner I also got the chance to patch things up with Rog (O'Gara) and Sexton, as I thought it was important to sort things out between us. I was sitting next to Simon Shaw at the dinner and he knows Rog well from the Lions tours. Rog was walking past our table and we looked at each other – as you do in those awkward situations – and we both decided to talk. We put our hands out to each other at more or less the same time so there was clearly a thought in both our heads at exactly the same time.

It turns out that he's a lot like me. He's an easygoing person and after chatting to him for a while I realised that we have very similar personalities. He's a good bloke, and I hope he now thinks better of me.

We talked about why we keep clashing on the pitch. And he said, 'You know why.' According to Rog, it all went back to the first time we played against each other in a Northampton-Munster Heineken Cup game. For his first kick I went running at him, trying to put him off. And after the game I went to shake his hand. He said, 'No, you show me some respect.' I was laughing in his face. What offended him was that he thought I was some Northerner who'd come from rugby league and had no idea about the game or who he was. He saw me as some idiot from another code coming over and giving him a load of stick. And I said, 'Yes, you're probably right.' I didn't think that at the time, however.

I think my relationship with Rog will be far better in the future now. We had a bit of a laugh and joke about things and I also got the chance to talk to Johnny Sexton, admitting to him that my attempts to put him off had backfired a little! I didn't apologise as such but I did admit that I gave him a lot of stick and he went on to get Man of the Match. The match could hardly have gone any worse for us and he was laughing about it.

The dinner broke up, but for us the formal side of the evening wasn't over because we still had to receive the RBS Six Nations trophy. We hadn't won the Grand Slam but we were still Six Nations champions, something no other England team has achieved since 2003.

Our spirits were pretty low on the bus from the ground, but

they were soon lifted when we saw the trophy and realised we were finally going to get our hands on it.

It was important that – as a team – we appreciated we had achieved something. It wasn't all doom and gloom.

I definitely look back on the Six Nations campaign with pride. It wasn't a failure just because we fell at the last hurdle and failed to win a Grand Slam. Losing to Ireland hurt and will hurt for many years to come, but we must also congratulate ourselves for what we did achieve. All other five teams in the championship would have swapped places with us. But it was still frustrating!

Straight after the whistle we didn't take consolation from the fact we were the first England team to win the title for eight years. But getting to the hotel, and seeing the trophy there in the lobby where they made the presentation, made us realise what we had achieved. It was something tangible.

Following the presentation a nightclub had been booked as it was the last game of the championship so we headed into the night. Most of the girlfriends weren't there but we mixed with the Irish lads a little. We'd all had quite a lot to drink – as you can imagine – and it wasn't long before I was thrown out for wrestling with former England player Matt Dawson. He came in and, as he had a terrible jacket on, both Dyl and I decided to wrestle him to the floor – which didn't go down too well with the bouncers. Dawson was also giving a lot of stick out so we decided to grab him and pin him down. It seemed like a good idea at the time!

The Grand Slam Dream Crushed

It was the end of a long and intense Six Nations and it's fair to say a few beers had been sunk at the post-match function. Not as many as when I won my first cap, but I was slightly the worse for wear roaming the streets of Dublin, a little on the vulnerable side.

I was on my own – which is unusual in itself – and I suddenly heard a familiar voice in the shape of Mike Tindall. Tins had been skipper for the first four games in the championship, missing out in the final one through injury. As everyone knows, he had been engaged to Zara Phillips for a while and the pair got married in the summer.

They hauled me into their cab, to save me from myself, I think. Being on my own in Dublin might not have been the best idea!

But I was so out of it that I'd forgotten who they were, and when the taxi stopped at some lights I leaped out and into McDonald's. It had all the hallmarks of a bad move. The last time I went into a burger bar in Ireland was after we played Munster and I got tackled into a table by a fan in Burger King.

At least this time I managed to stay on my feet (just) and this time Tins came running after me. There was a photographer following them and taking pictures of us eating all this food. I had no idea about all this but unfortunately the pictures ended up in the papers the next day. Tins was hiding his food, as he knew what was happening, but I was still stuffing my face. This photographer had been following them all night – it was something I just didn't realise happened.

Splashdown

We were due to have the players' court session back at Pennyhill Park when we landed from Dublin. This is one of rugby's great traditions, when all the fines are handed out from the championship. Probably one of the 'old school' players like Nick Easter would have been the judge, dishing it out. But the boys were so down and we needed to get back to our clubs on the Monday, so it was abandoned. There just didn't seem to be the collective energy in the squad for it.

In the days after the game Gerard Murphy, England's team psychologist, called me to talk about the game. And speaking to him made me realise how much I had lost the mental battle in the defeat to Ireland. He made it clear to me that we tensed up as the Ireland week went on. He asked me whether I thought the pressure and media attention that was put on me affected me and I said that I thought it did. When I reflect on that match it's clear the pressure had been building. I don't think I realised how heavily it weighed on my shoulders.

Gerard doesn't give advice in those situations. He just asks questions, which makes me realise exactly what has happened.

When I started my sessions with Gerard I was wary about telling him exactly what I thought in case it affected my chances of getting picked. But the longer I've stayed in the England squad, the more I've realised how important it is to be honest. When he first asked me whether I thought the pressure got to me, my instinct was to say no, but then I realised he was right, and that I needed to learn from situations like this, rather than brush them away.

If I'm not honest I won't get anywhere. His sessions really help and for any player to get the most out of them they have to be honest.

Gerard is in the dressing room before matches and I think he had picked up on the fact that I wasn't in the best frame of mind before we ran out against Ireland. But huge games like that are part of the learning experience for every international sportsman. You can't buy experience and my trip to Dublin showed me that. The key is to be better next time when the pressure comes on again.

I had been nominated for the Player of the Tournament alongside my English team-mates Toby Flood and James Haskell – although I'm not sure how Hask made the list! I totally forgot about it in the aftermath of the defeat by Ireland and in the end it went to Italy's Andrea Masi, as their win over France was one of the biggest shocks in years. Italy had an incredible tournament, beating the Grand Slam champions, France, so Andrea's award was well deserved, I'd say.

Ireland 24 England 8

Ireland
Tries: Bowe, O'Driscoll **Con:** Sexton **Pens:** Sexton 4
K Earls; T Bowe, B O'Driscoll (capt), G D'Arcy, A Trimble;
J Sexton, E Reddan; C Healy, R Best, M Ross,
D O'Callaghan, P O'Connell, S O'Brien, D Wallace, J Heaslip

Replacements: P Wallace for D'Arcy (79), R O'Gara for
Sexton (68), P Stringer for Reddan (71), S Cronin for Best
(78), T Court for Ross (58), L Cullen for O'Connell (78),
D Leamy for D Wallace (71)

England
Try: Thompson **Pen:** Flood
B Foden; C Ashton, M Banahan, S Hape, M Cueto;
T Flood, B Youngs; A Corbisiero, D Hartley, D Cole,
L Deacon, T Palmer, T Wood, J Haskell, N Easter (capt)
Replacements: D Strettle for Cueto (66), J Wilkinson for
Flood (51), D Care for Youngs (46), S Thompson for
Hartley (51), P Doran-Jones for Cole (51), T Croft for
Deacon (55), S Shaw for Palmer (27)
Sin-bin: Youngs (35)

Attendance: 51,000
Referee: B Lawrence (New Zealand)

7

Oh, When the Saints ...

I had started the 2010–11 season with my club, Northampton, on a high. I'd just helped England beat Australia in Sydney and although the Saints hadn't won a trophy the season before, we'd gone further than any other English club in the Heineken Cup by making the quarter-finals, and had also reached the semi-finals of the Guinness Premiership.

So I bounced into the end of pre-season training in a positive frame of mind.

Since we had got promoted from Division 1 in 2008, there was a general feeling we had been getting better and better. Players had come and gone but essentially it was the same group of lads that had served us so well in the past, something that always fills me with confidence. I don't like to see loads of changes – consistency is the key.

Splashdown

There was a bit of resentment left over from the previous campaign. That past season had gone well, but we ended it hearing Saracens singing their song at our ground after they had beaten us in the Premiership semi-finals. When we were sitting in our dressing room listening to them, many of us thought they were rubbing our noses in the defeat. It didn't go down too well with us lot. It was hard to take and it was certainly a motivation for me and many of the other lads when pre-season (and the hard work) started.

After a great 2009–10 season, it was important to recognise that life hadn't always been rosy for me in union. During the 2008–09 campaign I'd spent most of the time in Northampton's second team, playing just a few games in the first team. It just wasn't happening for me on the pitch.

They gave me a few chances but the coaches felt I was too much of a liability in defence and attack. They told me they didn't want to take that risk any more, which I wasn't happy with. They wanted to give Paul Diggin a chance.

I had never been in that position before, having played in the first team at Wigan from the age of eighteen. So I thought that within a couple of weeks I'd be back in the team. But that didn't prove the case and, apart from in Europe, I almost sat the whole year out.

However, I was top try-scorer in Europe that year.

The club did support me and helped me with training, but they needed to concentrate on the first team as we had just been promoted. It was a case of sometimes doing work on my own. Paul Grayson helped when I asked for it but it was still a long old year with the team doing well.

At that time it was hard to take and I was on the phone to my dad most nights. And even in the second team things weren't going right, so it was difficult for me.

Everything was pointing me back in the direction of rugby league but from this desperate situation I did get a crash course in some of the basics of union, which helped when I finally broke into the England set-up, late in 2009.

I hope I now look like I know what I'm doing. Dad was crucial in helping me through those tough times and convincing me to stay in union. He was keen on Northampton, despite the club's nickname of the Saints and our club song, 'When the Saints Go Marching In'.

That probably doesn't mean much to most people. It's a pretty inoffensive nickname as they go. But not in the eyes of a dyed-in-the-wool Wigan family: our biggest rugby league rivals were also the Saints – St Helens, our avowed enemies.

It may be just a song to some people, but it took me a long time to get used to hearing my fans singing a tune no Ashton could ever have brought themselves to utter.

My dad used to sit through that song over and over again in the Franklin's Gardens stands. He loved watching me play, he was proud of what I've achieved, and he never missed a home game – but there's no way he was ever going to sing 'When the Saints Go Marching In'.

All he ever wanted was to see his son in the hoops of Wigan –

then I went off to union . . . To his credit, he let me get on with it, but it took him time to come round. I reckon making the England squad might just have swung it in his mind.

I had arrived in union from Wigan rugby league with quite a lot of expectation on my shoulders. For every huge league success in union like Jason Robinson (another former Wigan RL player), there have been a number of failures and I didn't want to be another casualty on the list, especially as I was in the early stages of my career. The last thing I needed was a big failure on my record – I would have regretted that.

I knew it was going to be hard, but I didn't know quite how hard. There have been a few lads who have come over and, while they've not quite ended up as a nobody, have had to go back saying it wasn't right for them. I didn't want to be one of those people.

That's why when the 2010–11 season started it was so important to me to remember the difficult moments. I'd just won my first England caps and knew that if I was going to keep my career going in an upwards curve, it would all start at Northampton this season, one year from a World Cup. Get it right there and England selection would follow.

We believed that in this new season we would learn from those mistakes that left us just short the previous May and there was a belief among the players and coaches that this campaign would end with a trophy. We had played twice at Munster's ground, Thomond Park, and those sorts of experiences will naturally help you improve.

Oh, When the Saints . . .

We focused all year on doing the very best we could in every department and going one step better by winning something.

The seasons are long ones, especially with all the England fixtures. As I had gone to Australia with England I had about four weeks off in the summer, before returning to Northampton training where most of the lads had already almost completed their pre-season.

In one sense it's hard to arrive in the middle of what is everyone else's pre-season. It helps that other England players, like Courtney Lawes, Dylan Hartley and Ben Foden, are returning at the same time so you don't feel too out of place. But the rest of the squad had been getting used to each other and getting used to not having us around, so the first few days can be strange, as you're playing catch-up.

No allowances are made for the international players. We're expected to catch up with the other lads, and quickly. It's the same for any players who have been injured – no exceptions are made. I wasn't given a special programme because I had been away with England and that's exactly the way it should be. Fortunately, it didn't take too long to get up to speed.

I came back into the club at the start of August and the bonus was that I was glad to miss the heavy fitness work that Nick Johnston, Northampton's head of conditioning, had put the lads through in July. Torture is the only word to describe what he puts the lads through. He'll have put them through hill running and long-distance running with a 6 am start. The club have always started summer training early in the morning and although it's tough it has stood us in good stead so far. The theory goes that you train more effectively first thing in the morning and Nick puts that into practice.

We did it for the first time when we were preparing for life back in the Premiership. That was the worst and I still have nightmares about it now. He had us running ten kilometres, weights, breakfast, more weights, lunch and then wrestling or boxing. Nick would put us through strongman competitions, where you were pushing vans. I couldn't walk properly afterwards and when I was at home people would ask me 'What's wrong with you?' – that's how bad I looked! It's a total overload training programme, everyone being pushed to the maximum.

Nick's regime means that you can't totally relax even when you're on holiday because you know if you do you'll suffer when you get back. Nick gives us programmes when we're on our summer holidays. He advises us to have two weeks completely off and then the hellish routine begins, which is very tough after all we've gone through the season before.

Some people do over-indulge in the summer and that can make pre-season training tough. Nonetheless, all of us know that it is a very necessary part of being a rugby player. This was particularly the case when we came up from Division 1 and had to get ready for the Premiership.

We try to persuade Nick to slow down sometimes, but he doesn't listen and sometimes it's no fun to be there with him. But we all know he knows his stuff and his objective is to make us a better team, so we accept it. In the summer of 2010 because I was away with England I only ended up doing a week of it, but it felt like seven anyway.

There was no problem with the other lads, even though we turned up when the hard stuff was almost finished. When that was me completing the whole of pre-season and watching the England lads come back, I used to think, 'I want that to be me. I want to work extra hard in these fitness sessions so I can make it at Test level.'

Obviously a few try it on and feign injury to get out of the fitness work. Foden is sometimes a prime suspect – I see him running holding his back, which is always a good one!

All the players are doing exactly the same programme so it means some of the heavier lads find it a real struggle to cope.

Sometimes I will finish and then go back and help Soane Tonga'uiha, which means he might go easier on me in the wrestling. In fact, I'll do anything to try to avoid Soane in the wrestling – he normally manages to get hold of me and throw me around the gym. But if that happens my tactic is just to let it happen. There is no point fighting it – better to get it over as quickly as possible.

You do try to pick your targets. I tried to match myself up with Shane Geraghty when he was at the club. Later in the year when we started wrestling with England, Ben Youngs injured his knee and was out for a few weeks. John Brake, who now has a contract with England Sevens, and Bruce Reihana, now at Bordeaux Bègles, were two to avoid when it came to training. Both are fitness freaks and love training. As Bruce is so tough and loves the physical side I used to try to make him train with the forwards so he didn't break any of us – he's a crazy Kiwi.

Nick has managed to find the biggest hill in the area for us to run up and although sometimes there is talk of us doing some things that are a little more fun, like speed golf, it never seems to happen. Nick prefers getting us to run around with weights on our back. The best day out we get is kayaking around this huge lake or doing a ten-kilometre bike ride around Pitsford. That is Nick's idea of down time for us – I can tell you that not even that is much fun . . .

In all seriousness I enjoy Nick's work – in a strange way – as I enjoy getting fit for the new season. I think that's because of the way my dad brought me up. My dad used to take me out for ten-kilometre runs all the time, even though when I was young I used to trail miles behind him.

I don't know any other clubs in the Aviva Premiership who train as hard as we do. We don't co-ordinate our work with England as we believe 'Nick knows best' but I think they do let the England management know what we are doing.

It was completely different to what I would have done at Wigan. For one thing, with rugby league being a summer sport, the pre-season is done in winter. I was speaking to Shontayne Hape about this and he reckons he could have done twenty years of union if he had started when he was a teenager, but league has completely knackered him out. He says his knees are damaged from league – but I think it's the other way round. It's just as physical and just as much hard work in union.

Fitness-wise in league you're training for ten yards and back, so there are a lot of short, sharp sessions. We were constantly doing shuttles in order to build that explosive running. But union is so much faster than even a year or two ago – it's definitely changing.

Before Northampton hit the domestic campaign, we had a trip to southern France to play against Dax, although we stayed just outside Biarritz. They put us out of town in an area on our own so there wasn't much chance for socialising. At that time we counted the game as a training session so we didn't stop training a couple of days beforehand as we would normally. The training just kept on going.

It's not what you call fun, as an amateur team would enjoy a pre-season tour, but we did manage to fit in a session of white-water rafting. We had three boats but it soon turned into chaos with everyone fighting! It was three-and-a-half hours of non-stop fighting, trying to stop the other boats winning. How no one got injured I don't know. Even the instructors were getting knocked off the boats so I think they stopped it early, just to get us off.

Our coaches, Jim Mallinder and Dorian West, got involved 100 per cent. When it comes to an event like that they're like one of us, so everyone was trying to get them out of the boat, although Westy takes a bit of shifting. Westy used to be in the police force and he has all these police techniques he tries on people – it was a case of anything goes.

There is obviously a time and a place for the coaches to create some distance between themselves and the players, and I think at Northampton they get it right. They came out with us at the end of the season when we lost the Heineken Cup final. There are times when it works to have us all mixing socially and that was one example – they're pretty good at working that sort of stuff out.

Paul Grayson is the coach I work with most closely. He was the guy who signed me so we had a close working relationship right from the start and that has stuck. He's a Lancashire lad and he's always the one I've gone and spoken to if I've had any problems. He has always been the one to help.

I speak to Grayse about the good and the bad as he has been there since I came over from rugby league and has been through the ups and the downs with me. He's always the person I watch the match videos with. Grayse knows his stuff and I've been grateful for his input over the years. He's a very knowledgeable coach and his time in the England team has been invaluable to me. He's always spoken to my family and been supportive since I joined from league. He helped me when I came across and he was the one who helped me get involved with England.

The Dax game was hard work as we were all running round like headless chickens. It was almost like a kids' game again.

We lost, Paul Diggin's back went almost as soon as we

kicked off, and Scott Armstrong, another of our wingers, injured the ligaments in his ankle, so it wasn't the best of matches. They had to send a minibus back early with the injured lads and it was almost full!

Back in England, before the onset of the season, we played Nottingham and Viadana, most of the first team missing the match against Nottingham. We took Viadana a lot more seriously because that game came only one week before the Aviva Premiership season began. We needed to start looking like a well-honed Premiership team.

The season proper kicked off in exactly the way I would have liked, with a massive game. We played Leicester at home and to top it off we beat our biggest rivals, by 27–19. We started really well as we always do. I think we've opened the past few seasons so well because our pre-season is so good. Everyone was fresh and we felt a good team.

I don't think you hit top form until five or six weeks in, because you're feeling your way. But it's the same for everyone so there are no excuses, and for this season we were well prepared.

Leicester have had the best team in England for a while and because we are close geographically they're the ones we want to beat most of all. It's the local derby and they have what we want – trophies.

I get on better with the Leicester contingent after being with them for England. Meeting them through playing for your country helps a lot and makes you understand that the way people are on the pitch isn't necessarily how they are in reality.

The game also gave Soane the chance to believe he could be the leading try-scorer at the club! I didn't score but made one of his two tries. He went from two to five tries pretty quickly in the season and was giving me a lot of chat in training about how he was going to end up with more tries than me.

He always seems to score a few early tries – I think because he's always fit at the start of the season, having endured Nick's pre-season of hell. Perhaps he needs to stay on pre-season a bit longer and maybe he'd score a few more. Or maybe he likes playing with the sun on his back?

Soane is an amazing character. He's a good friend but I probably don't see him as much as I might because he has a young family. I remember we were at Treviso once, in three feet of snow, and someone hit him on the head with a snow-ball and he wasn't happy at all. He thought it was me and started chasing me around a car park.

We had a snowball each and both 'agreed' to drop them. When I dropped mine he charged at me and started swinging. I landed in a thorn bush and he was on top of me (all 20-stone plus of him). Luckily Nacho (Ignacio Fernández Lobbe) had seen what had happened and he came flying in and cleared him out textbook style and got him off me. If Nacho hadn't got there I don't know what would have happened. Perhaps we'd still be there now! Soane apologised afterwards and there were no hard feelings. It was just one of those things that happen when snowballs start flying about!

Everyone at Northampton appreciates that it's much better

to have Soane on our side than against us, so we were all delighted when he pulled out of that move to Saracens. He looked all set to go but luckily for us had a change of heart. I think he was committed to going but at the last minute realised he was settled in Northampton, with his family, and it wasn't something he was ready to do. So he and the club sorted out their differences and they were able to persuade him back round.

Players tend not to try to talk team-mates out of a move like that: we tend to leave it up to the individual. Players moving on is a fact of life, after all. But we gave Soane a load of stick in training about it, all good-natured but with a serious edge. I spoke to Soane and it seemed that, although the situation wasn't managed very well, it got changed round and everyone was happy. Well, apart from Saracens.

After winning at home to Leicester, we headed to Harlequins with a big change of tactics that Jim thought had hampered us in the past. We had a terrible record at Quins and Jim was convinced it was down to the fact that we always planned a big night out in London on the back of the trip.

Jim believed the plans and the night out had been a distraction for us in the past, so this time we were back on the bus after the match. To be fair we had played so badly the last two times at Quins that he was right to change something. Even in the 2009–10 season when we were playing well, we'd gone to Quins and played terribly.

We've got to know Jim over the years and we know if there

is leeway or not if he says things in a certain way. This time he left us in no doubt that it was a decision we couldn't challenge. He told us all in the team meeting, when he announced the team.

He always announces the team at nine thirty on a Wednesday morning, in front of the whole team and the academy lads. He'll walk in with his bit of paper, but Fodes and I have a joke because most of the time the team is exactly the same as the week before so we're convinced there is nothing actually on the paper. It's the way he says it – 15, Foden, 14, Ashton, 13, Clarke, 12, Downey – it's like a little rhyme. Fodes and I can nail it every single time.

In this particular week he didn't say outright that we weren't allowed to go out after the game, he just said, 'Everyone is back on the bus' after the match. None of the players disagreed with Jim. We had no intention of going out afterwards anyway this season, our only concern was winning that game.

I think the Quins game just came at a better time for us in 2010. It was the second game in and we'd just beaten Leicester, whereas the previous fixture was right in the middle of a tough season and it's easy to have a dip then. We just made sure there weren't going to be any mistakes this time – it was important we got it right. Winning there (20–16) for the first time in six years was a big day for us, but even then it was very close.

Danny Care, the Quins scrum-half and my good England mate, could have won it for them right at the end. They should have scored in the corner but somehow Fodes held Joe Marler up. Then Danny broke off the back of the scrum in the dying minutes and sold a dummy. I fell for the dummy but recovered enough to dive and hit the ball out of his hand as he went over. He was very upset about it and I was laughing. Even though the referee said 'Play on', I just stood there laughing and patting Danny on the head.

The game also marked my first try of the season. I never set myself targets for a season but I expect to score tries, that's my job. It's always something I think will happen and I hope I don't go too many games without scoring one.

I don't get any financial bonus for scoring tries, which I think is right. If people start getting that sort of incentive they can get greedy, which isn't the way you want a player in a rugby team to be. That would distract me. It's a team game and it's all about the team winning, so I don't see why I or anyone else should get paid to score tries.

Some people have win bonuses and other sorts of bonuses in their contract but I don't because I earn a straight salary. We get team bonuses for how far we get in particular competitions – that is more of a team-doing-well bonus, so I don't mind that.

We were feeling great after those first two games and it continued into the Bath home game, before the season came to a stuttering halt for me just three games in when I was injured in the match.

That was a night of great celebration for the pack as they

took Bath apart in the scrum. The 2010–11 season was all about our pack and how well they were playing and I think that started with this game, as they were in immense form. ESPN had come in to cover rugby, Martin Johnson was in the crowd, and it was our first Friday-night home game in I don't know how long, so there seemed to be a special atmosphere around Franklin's Gardens that night. Bath had also started very well and the defeat clearly rocked them as they stayed on the pitch for a long time afterwards dissecting the game.

It was a great night for the club but not for me as someone landed on my foot, injuring my toes, banging two bones together. I tried to play on but could feel my boot filling up with my foot, so I knew I had to get off.

In the event I was out of action for four weeks, which was a real shame. At one stage I thought it was going to threaten my place in the England team for the Autumn Internationals, not that it was my primary concern. I know some people say players save themselves for England, but I've never thought that way. When I came off I was hoping to play against Saracens a week later, and the game against New Zealand for England on 6 November wasn't a factor. Northampton is my home and where I belong – the Saints are my first priority. I want to play for them every week.

To think anything else would be insulting to everyone at the Saints, particularly the fans.

Injuries are a fact of life. They will always come sooner or later and when they do only two things matter: how you deal with the injury, and how you can come back stronger. Focusing on coming back stronger is my way of trying to turn a negative into a positive. In this instance it could have been a lot worse but ultimately it was only four weeks, so I can consider myself lucky.

I love to run and I love to be able to train, so it does bother me when an injury comes along that stops me doing that. However, the rehab they have now is so flexible that you can keep working hard almost no matter what your injury is. I believe as long as I listen to the medical staff at Northampton and England then the injury won't have as detrimental effect as it might have had in the past. I was very fortunate to have no injuries at all in the 2009–10 season, so I suppose it was inevitable that one was coming in this campaign.

After a great win like the one against Bath (31–10), we would normally all go out as a squad in Northampton to celebrate, but with my injury I didn't join them this time.

People in Northampton are pretty good when we go out though sometimes they can get a bit difficult if we've lost. I see going out as a way of celebrating, so when we lose I don't see why you should. Finals are probably the exception to this rule, but not after a league match.

At Northampton we were very lucky to have Keith Barwell as our chairman. This was his last season in the job, but he has been a huge factor in how well the club have done in recent years. I don't have a huge amount of contact with him on a day-to-day basis – he's more like a fan. He doesn't get involved in anything else. But there's no doubt the club is fortunate to have him at the top, and his family are leading the proposals to redevelop the ground which will make Franklin's Gardens even better, with another new stand, behind the posts.

At Wigan the chairman, Maurice Lindsay, used to come in the dressing room, especially if we'd had a bad day, but Keith never used to do that. Maurice would sometimes let us know exactly how he felt. 'You're making a mockery of Wigan,' he'd shout. Wigan coach Ian Millward also used to get mad at us after matches.

Jim and Westy are pretty good when we've lost. I can't remember a game when we've been completely battered by them. Sometimes it's needed straight after a game, especially if the simple things have been going wrong. If I knew I'd done something wrong in a game it wouldn't worry me if someone said it. But that's not how Jim is. Jim can get angry when he needs to but on the whole he's pretty calm. He'll usually give it the weekend to think about it, and look back on events a few days later rather than try to put things right through emotion.

Jim is a very considered coach. He'll take time over every decision and weigh up all the options before making any calls. He's not one to come in the dressing room screaming and shouting.

Our good start to the season was soon halted by another defeat to Saracens. I was injured but I went along as a fan. I didn't go with the lads but with Melissa. I enjoy watching rugby and regard being injured as a chance to look on from the sidelines.

I didn't go into the dressing room before the game, but I did text good-luck messages to a few of the lads. One of the texts was to Digger (Paul Diggin), who took my place in the team. As a group of wings we get on well at Northampton.

It was agony watching the Saints lose to Saracens at Vicarage Road, 24–17. Sometimes it's difficult to watch, especially when things are going wrong. I try to sit away from everyone else and would never shout, rant and rave as I'm not a big fan of that. Some of the lads say they don't like watching rugby, but I've never understood that. I love to watch it – as long as the boys perform.

I left with five minutes to go – when I could see we couldn't win – but when I got back to the car I was delighted to hear on the radio that Digger had scored a late try in the corner to get us a bonus point.

I would never want to go into the dressing room after a game I'm not playing in, especially if we had lost. I don't know how people would take it. Dyl might do it but then he is cap-tain – he feels he should. But personally I would worry that the players would say 'What's he doing in here?' if I wasn't playing.

After Saracens, we took on the Premiership new boys, Exeter Chiefs, who had just been promoted. Many people saw Exeter as one of the weaker teams but as their season showed they were far from that. And I've always thought if a team is written off they can be the most dangerous opponents of all because they have nothing to lose.

We were winning pretty easily, but we must have switched off, because they came flying back into it and almost nicked the game, so we were very annoyed at the way it turned out. It finished 27–21.

The match gave one of Northampton's old boys, Chris Budgen, the chance to come back to Franklin's Gardens. He's a Kiwi prop who juggles playing professional rugby with an army career that has taken him to Iraq and Afghanistan – incredible really.

He was at Northampton in my early days there, when we were in Division 1. Most people call him Budgie but for me he'll always be Chicken Bro because he's a Kiwi and if you gave him any banter he'd make this weird noise, like a chicken, and call everyone 'Bro'. I'm not sure who made up the name, someone at Northampton said it was because he loved KFC, and it has stuck!

I remember when we were in Division 1 he used to leave us and go off to the army. 'What's going on with him?' I used to wonder. He's a real character. Rugby union is a sport for all shapes and sizes and Chicken Bro shows that with style.

I didn't see him after the game because I was so annoyed about nearly losing the match that I went home straightaway, but I'm sure if I had caught up with him he'd have made some chicken noises.

At the time, the battle was still going on between Shane

Geraghty and Stephen Myler for the number 10 shirt at Northampton. Shaneo was in for this game with Bruce Reihana kicking. Jim likes people he can rely on and if you want reliability then Stephen is your man.

However, there is no doubt Shaneo has some flair and during the course of the season you'd often see him create a try out of nothing. It was only a few years ago that he was doing that for England. But it's no good if you can't keep it consistent, which is why Jim went with Mylo, and Shaneo ended up joining Brive. Mylo is steady as a rock and proved so all season. Mr Cool is what I call him – it doesn't seem that anything can rattle him.

After five Premiership games, we had chalked up four wins – achieving the target we had set ourselves. Those targets are easy when you play in blocks but the English season certainly has a challenging structure and now we were about to move into the Heineken Cup for two rounds.

We also had a big change at tighthead prop in the course of the season, which for a Premiership club is very unusual. With the way contracts are structured now from season to season, it's very rare, almost unheard of really, for a player to move to another club during the season.

In football they have a transfer system, but that hasn't really emerged in rugby union and on the whole players only move when their contracts have concluded. Well, in this season the unusual became reality for us with Euan Murray moving from Northampton to Newcastle.

Splashdown

The issue centred around Euan's religious beliefs, which meant he refused to play on a Sunday. We had been together in the side since my first season in union in 2007–08 in Division 1, and it was clear Euan was becoming more and more religious over the years. You would see him in the town centre giving out leaflets, and when he signed autographs he would put a Bible reference underneath.

Euan is a great bloke and, as he proved on the 2009 Lions tour, and again in the 2011 World Cup, a great player. I was sorry to see him go. As far as I'm concerned it's a case of 'each to their own' but the selection issue was making it difficult for him to be part of the squad as we seem to have more and more matches on a Sunday. Euan put himself out of the picture by not being available on Sundays, finally moving to a club who play their home games on a Friday night.

I didn't know Euan that well but as he was moving in and out of the team during the season it coincided with the emergence of Brian Mujati, the Zimbabwean tighthead who played for South Africa.

Brian is a very quiet bloke who doesn't like to talk to people he's not familiar with, so it took him a while to settle in at Northampton. Euan's departure allowed Brian to come to the fore in the tighthead position and he started to form a formidable partnership with Dyl and Soane in the front row. Those three became the starting front row and took us into the Heineken Cup.

It's good going into Europe, especially when you have been

doing well in the Aviva Premiership, but the movement between competitions does take some getting used to.

However, the upside is that it's challenging and better for you as players to test yourself against different teams. And it's all club rugby at the end of the day, so it's not too massive a change.

There is a slightly different buzz around the club when it comes to the Heineken Cup and clearly the pressure is greater because everyone knows you can't really afford to lose any games in the group stages, especially in the first round.

I came back from injury for the first Heineken Cup game against Castres and we started with an unconvincing 18–14 win. It was a difficult game. We thought it would be easier than it was as they hadn't won away yet that season. I was most worried about getting my leg right that week because I hadn't trained properly. I wanted to be absolutely certain that my foot was good to play.

From Castres we completed the first part of our Heineken Cup campaign with a trip to Murrayfield to play Edinburgh. It was odd playing in front of 6,000 people in a stadium that holds almost 70,000. There were three and a half stands empty and more than half the fans who attended had travelled from Northampton.

The artificial atmosphere threw us off a little and Edinburgh started very well, playing an expansive style that we struggled to contain at times. They threw the ball around and it took us half an hour to get into the game. But once we were in and ahead I never thought we would ever lose.

Splashdown

It was in this match that I suffered the embarrassment of having the ball knocked out of my hand as I dived over the line. But it was a good tackle, rather than a loose carry on my part, that was responsible. As I was getting the ball over, one of their players managed to dislodge it, something that hasn't happened before and won't happen again. I'd like to stress – I didn't drop the ball!

The most important thing, however, was that we were two out of two and the trip to Scotland gave me the chance to see Edinburgh forwards coach Tom Smith, who I had played with at Northampton in Division 1. Tom is a real old-school rugby player, who had an amazing career with Northampton, Scotland and the Lions. I've seen him get trampled on the head a few times and get up and laugh at the opposition. We were happy we went all that way up north and won 31–27. And the support we got from the Saints fans that day was amazing.

Travelling away isn't something that seems to be part of the culture at every rugby union club but it makes a huge difference to the players to see your own supporters greeting you at away matches when you run out. Particularly that day: the Saints fans should take a bow for the effort it took to follow us.

Helping people with away travel and encouraging them to follow the Saints all over Europe is part of what Keith Barwell is all about. He can see the huge benefit in it.

In the village where I live just outside Northampton, people recognise me and come up to me, but it's 100 per cent supportive. Even when we lose everyone is saying 'Bad luck' rather than berating me for losing. It's due to being at such a prominent club, I suppose – being part of such a big thing for the town.

The trip to Wasps next up was an important game for us, because it was the last game before we all went off with England, so I wanted to ensure we put in a good performance. All week we spoke about how we had never won there, and it was our chance this season to put that right.

Before we kicked off, Dyl made the point in the huddle that some of the lads were leaving to play Test rugby and we should leave Northampton with a big performance before we joined up with England. It was going to be the last Northampton match for some of us and it was important to leave on a high note, which luckily we did. The forwards again were unbelievable in that game. We absolutely battered them and on the pitch you could hear the Wasps guys arguing among themselves, which is unusual to see. We won 37–10 and it was a huge thing for Northampton to achieve.

As soon as that game kicked off we scored two tries pretty quickly and with the forwards pushing them around it was happy days for all of us. Wasps had a potent pair of wings in David Lemi and Tom Varndell, but they didn't get enough ball to do too much damage. It was one of those days when we were in charge for the whole match.

I scored a try against Wasps but Soane scored twice, keeping up his amazing record for getting over the whitewash. I've tried so many times to get on the back of those mauls. The forwards say 'Yes, of course', but when it comes to it they don't let me – they just keep hold of the ball themselves!

It's my job to score tries so it does get into the back of your mind when you go on a bad run. I hadn't scored for a few weeks so it was great to finally get over the line, after a lovely grubber by Mylo. Grayse came into the dressing room after the match and said 'It's great to have you back.' Cheeky so-and-so!

In the Dallaglio era, Wasps were the ones challenging and often beating Leicester, and I hope we (and Saracens) have taken over that mantle, even if we haven't yet won the Aviva Premiership or Heineken Cup since 2000.

As Wasps have slipped down the table, we've gone up and this was a very pleasing win, especially because of the way we did it with the forwards just battering them.

After the match we saw former Wigan legend Shaun Edwards, who is the Wasps defence coach. I grew up watching Shaun on the terraces at Central Park, although he's a bit older than me so we never played at the same time. I might have asked him for an autograph but that is about it – that's as close as it came.

At Wasps you have to walk from the dressing rooms across the pitch to the post-match food. Whenever we went there and lost, once we had got changed and crossed the pitch forty-odd minutes after the match, Shaun would be in his vest and shorts doing coat-hangers. These are a set of shuttle-running fitness exercises where you start in the middle of the pitch and run to the corners, in a coat-hanger shape.

Oh, When the Saints . . .

I know Shaun is a fitness fanatic and a bit crazy with his gym work, but I noticed he did it when we lost. Yet funnily enough when we came out of the dressing room this time – having won – Shaun was nowhere to be seen. I don't know if that was to do with them getting battered or not, but I know he wasn't out there that day.

I speak to Shaun whenever I get a chance. I've bumped into him in Wigan a few times. He's a good guy and rang me when my dad died, which I appreciated. I thought it was good of him to take the time to offer his condolences. We have another emotional connection in that my brother's best friend died in the same car as Shaun's brother died in a few years ago, so we're pretty close although we haven't met that many times.

From the Wasps game, with Dyl's words ringing in our ears, it was time to head off to play for England in the Investec November Internationals. I love playing for England. Running out at Twickenham, playing in the Six Nations, and taking part in the Rugby World Cup are three of the reasons I moved from rugby league to union. However, there is one notable downside. Unlike in football, where the Premier League programme is suspended when England play, in rugby the Aviva Premiership carries on when we play in the Autumn Internationals or Six Nations.

So it was heart-breaking for the Northampton boys who were with England to watch on from a distance as the Saints went on a losing run while we were playing in the Six Nations. Now I'm not saying things were going wrong because myself,

Fodes, Tom Wood and Dyl weren't around, with Courtney Lawes being injured. But that didn't stop us feeling for the boys back home.

It's an almost hidden part of the game, as people don't tend to talk about it too much. I know it frustrates the hell out of supporters because they tell me. Supporters buy their season tickets to watch the best players and for chunks of the season they can't.

Of course we keep in touch with the Saints players when we're with England, but it's hard seeing the results coming in.

I will text or call a few of the boys and on my day off from England – which is often Thursday – I'll try to make a point of calling in at the club and see the lads. When you do that you tend to get a bit of stick – naturally – but I like to show my face when I'm back in Northampton. Most of the England boys do that. I think it's important to keep in touch with the Saints lads and support them, even when I'm away with England.

I also speak to Grayse about the England game, how I've played, how things are going or how training is shaping up. I trust his opinion on my England performances. He knows a few of the personalities who are with England, so he is a good sounding board for me.

England Under-20 player Jamie Elliott came in on the wing when I was away with England and he did really well. I'll try to make more time going forward to work with him but in this particular season – which was so busy – it was more about just wishing him well and saying well done.

Oh, When the Saints . . .

In one way it is great for guys like Jamie to get a chance when we are away. They are the stars of the future after all and exposure to the Aviva Premiership will bring dividends in the seasons to come.

8

Christmas and Beyond

After the November Tests, I came back into the Northampton team with a bang, as we were almost straight back into the Heineken Cup.

In December you play the same team in your pool on consecutive weekends and for us that was Cardiff Blues. It's something I've never heard of before in any sport and it can be really hard work facing the same team back-to-back – it makes it twice as hard.

I suppose it was the England–Wales rivalry but the first game, which was at home, was pretty fiery and ensured a few leftovers for the return match in Cardiff the following weekend. We won both of them, but they were very difficult days.

Christmas and Beyond

I understand why back-to-back games are quite fun for supporters, TV and the organisers, but from a player's perspective they're not popular. The problem is that stuff from one week is carried on.

Playing them again so quickly left people even more wound up and in some cases distracted, but winning both games (23–15 and 23–19) was massive for us.

I scored, which was great. Not just because I like scoring but because being away with England for a while made me think I owed the lads a little, so I wanted to repay them.

Sometimes it's hard to step back into club rugby. You have to learn the calls again and it was a very big, high-pressurised match. There's no messing about or easing your way back in gently when you have to play a Heineken Cup game. In fact, the first training session was difficult as the ground was hard and Jim lost his head with us at one point. Myself, Jimmy Downey and Fodes were messing around, not concentrating, and Jim was calling us 'Big time', giving us stick.

There is no sense of working your way back into the team – if you come back thinking you're better than when you went away, or give that impression, the team makes sure those feelings go pretty quickly!

The main thing was getting the home win, as we hosted Cardiff Blues first. It was a bit rowdy but we won before making it four out of four in our pool the following weekend.

In the second match in particular there were cheap shots

going in all over the pitch. Dyl got gouged by Richie Rees – who was subsequently banned for twelve weeks after the judicial officer said it was reckless but not intentional – and Courtney got hit with a high tackle by Xavier Rush, who got sent off. There was a lot going on in that game, almost enough for a whole season.

The Cardiff Blues games had taken a lot out of us so it was great to let our hair down a bit at our club's Christmas party, which took place on the Monday following our win in Wales. The Christmas party is always a bit of a riot, and wonderful for team spirit.

I used to be on the social committee, so I was at the centre of the action. Well, planning the action anyway. But I resigned from it recently. Not that I had a fallout, I'd just had enough. One of the main reasons I stepped down was because I like surprises and when you organise an event you know exactly what is going to happen, so it takes some of the fun out of it.

I still get some influence in what we do, however, because Dylan Hartley is still on it – he has to be as captain – so I can make sure I get my views across. We have Secret Santa every year, as you might expect. I usually receive something like a handbag, which is meant for Melissa but at the same time serves to take the mickey out of me. It tends to be something not that useful, shall we say. I got Jamie Elliott in the draw, so I went for the obvious and got him some acne cream. You can see the level we're talking about . . .

The Christmas party always has a fancy-dress theme and

this time it was Alter Ego Superheroes. As usual it was carnage. I went as Super Rastaman and looked pretty sharp, I thought.

The party is just for the players, including the academy lads – no coaches or partners allowed. We always start off at the Crooked Hooker, which is the famous bar at Franklin's Gardens run for former players of the club, and it goes on from there.

Once we were rocking in the Crooked Hooker, a decorated double-decker bus turned up to take us on a pub crawl. It's our big blow-out of the year.

It was great, although you have to remember this is more than thirty pretty big lads in one confined space so accidents will happen – all breakages are paid for!

The night ended in a nightclub in Northampton but I think that is probably the end of it now. We've done it two years in a row and I'm not sure anyone could stand a third.

It was time to focus back on the rugby.

I hate to miss any matches but in some ways it was good news for me when our match against Gloucester was called off over Christmas. It was the first Christmas for me without my dad so I was relieved to get the chance to go home and see the family.

It was hard to be there at home without him. Under usual circumstances I would have gone home to Wigan before Christmas and returned to Northampton on Christmas Day to play in the Gloucester match the following day. Even though it was the first Christmas without my dad, I wouldn't have considered asking Jim Mallinder for the day off, especially as I could go up to Wigan beforehand, but in the end it was nice to be there on Christmas Day, without the pressure of having to leave early.

My dad would have gone mad had I asked Jim, and in fact my family were ready to continue the family tradition my dad started of all the family coming to watch the rugby on Boxing Day.

In the end I stayed up in Wigan for the whole of Christmas with Melissa. It was a pretty tough time without Dad but you have to get on with it and spend as much time as you can with family. Dad was a churchgoer and on Christmas Eve he used to attend a Catholic church service. I never would go then but I did on Christmas Day, mainly because Dad wanted us to go. He'd normally make me go on Christmas Day, even if I had gone out the night before. This year, though, as Mum was on her own, I went on Christmas Eve as well.

We still had fun, even if we all missed Dad greatly. We had lots of friends around, and no one had to really say what was missing. We all knew who should have been there.

On Boxing Day the game for the Ashton family was always Wigan v St Helens, a real family tradition. But now with rugby league moving to a summer sport that has gone – it's not the same any more. So there was no sport for us. Christmas and New Year aren't the same for professional sportsmen and even though our Boxing Day game was off, I was soon back in training mode as we were playing Harlequins on New Year's Day.

Christmas and Beyond

You can't do what most people do on New Year's Eve. I couldn't do anything more strenuous than taking Melissa to watch the fireworks at the London Eye, and coming back straight after to get beaten 16–13 at home by Quins the next day, which was a shocker for us.

It was a massive surprise, being our first home defeat since the previous May, and it was doubly annoying because we knew there was no need to lose that game. I'm not sure whether we got distracted because it was that time of year, but they annoyed us for the whole game. The Cardiff Blues games had also taken a lot out of us and Quins came to disrupt us. Even when they had two players in the sin-bin we couldn't get the ball off them. Danny Care scored a lucky try off a charge-down and we didn't get the chance to knock the ball out of his hands this time.

I suppose it was retribution after we had gone to their place and won, but losing the game really bothered me. It was our worst home defeat for a while and to compound my misery I injured my quad muscle so was also a bit distracted by that.

Northampton's New Year hangover continued as we lost to Leicester, 27–16. I pretty much knew I wasn't fit but I was aware of how much the Leicester game means to our fans and the club, so I wanted to be out there and I managed to convince myself I was fit.

Before the game I didn't warm up enough because I was worried I would overdo it. I just didn't want to miss it – who would want to miss a game like that? But in the first minute the injury went again. Fodes made a break to score and I went with him and as soon as I went to sprint I tore it more, so while I was celebrating with him I was thinking 'Oh no'.

I tried to carry on and got to about twenty-five minutes into the match before having to come off. It was another setback and I thought we were really unlucky to lose, as the lads played well.

We weren't so down about the loss because we felt we had bounced back well from an awful defeat at home to Quins to put in a good performance against Leicester – one that should have brought a victory. I think if we had produced the performance we managed that day against any other team in the league we would have won the game. It just happened it was Leicester at Welford Road and that is why we had a loss on our record.

That injury cost me another three weeks of my club season, which took me into the Six Nations. I missed the Castres game away in the Heineken Cup, and just got myself ready for the trip to Cardiff with England, for the start of the Six Nations.

Westy was giving me a bit of stick, saying I was saving myself for England, but it was only banter as he knows I would never do that. I just wanted to make sure the quad was right. My desire to play for Northampton took me on the field at Leicester, where I made it worse. Just as in November, it was very hard to be away from the club, with the other England boys.

This time the lads struggled in the Aviva Premiership, which made it even harder for me to watch, and being with England meant I couldn't get down to the club as often as I would have liked. The games were tough to watch.

We carried on getting beaten, at home to Saracens (29–15) and then a big defeat at Bath. The 38–8 loss at Bath was embarrassing for the team, the club, the supporters – everyone. When Bath came to us earlier in the season we hammered them, but this time they turned the tables and it hurt.

I don't think the problems were down to the fact that the England players weren't there, but it was a tough time for the club as a whole. The lads had played well in November so why not in February and March? Looking at the pack for instance it was very strong, but sometimes it's down to the mindset – once you lose it can start to slip away from you. It's a time of the year when some clubs are getting on a run, playing really well, so it can be tough if you start the period badly.

We lost at home to Gloucester, 18–16, then at the start of March lost 30–9 at Exeter to record a sixth successive Premiership defeat. I rang a few of the players, like Roger Wilson and Jimmy Downey, to offer my support but they couldn't really explain it either. They thought we had lost confidence.

The structure of the league means there are play-offs so all is not lost. But relying on the play-offs only lasts so long. These are proud men who don't like to lose once, let alone six times in a row and some of those by emphatic margins.

The players were doing their best to try and understand why things were going wrong so they could turn things around.

But sometimes when you're in a losing run it's hard to get out of it. Even at home we were losing.

We did play some of the top teams, like Sarries and Gloucester, which wasn't in our favour, and we managed to scrape a win at Leeds Carnegie (23–13), before we all returned from the Six Nations.

I was pleased to see the boys win before we returned as we didn't want it to seem that the England players coming back would suddenly make everything okay. That sort of sentiment is not what rugby is all about. So it was good that the boys picked up a win without us. It's a long, punishing season in which there will be downs as well as ups and we never doubted they'd be able to pull out of this slump.

When all the England players got back into the side it was time to switch straight to the Heineken Cup knockout stage, although we knew that as we had qualified as the top seed in the competition we'd get a home draw.

We also knew that the match wouldn't be played at Franklin's Gardens. Heineken Cup regulations mean that Franklin's Gardens is slightly too small to host a quarter-final, so the decision was taken to move the game to Milton Keynes where the MK Dons play football.

It was strange to go there but it did give us the chance to showcase rugby in a new town, which was near enough to Northampton so not too inconvenient for our fans. It was exciting to go and play somewhere I'd never been before and the players took the decision the right way – positively.

Christmas and Beyond

We got the chance to train there a few times before the match and, after going out in Munster in the quarter-finals the year before, we saw this as our chance to go one or two steps further. We took a lot of confidence from our perfect record in the pool stages, from winning at places like Cardiff and Castres, and we used that belief and confidence in the quarter-final against Ulster.

Ulster had scraped in on the final day of the pool matches, and it was their first time in the quarter-finals for a while, which made them dangerous opponents. They're a very well-supported club with a great Heineken Cup tradition, so we knew we'd have to be on song to beat them.

And beat them we did, in what turned out to be an extremely tough game. Soane got back on the scoreboard early on, which settled us down, and although they managed to get on top for a while, we were able to pull clear to win 23–13. For a spell I was thinking this game could go either way here, but we came up with a brilliant try to put us on the way to the semis.

Lee Dickson's amazing try was undoubtedly the turning point. It was a score I was involved in and which saw the ball go through several pairs of hands before Lee dived over. I remember Jon Clarke giving Lee the ball and he was screaming for it back, but it was never coming back.

Perhaps Lee's secret comes from his love of a certain sweet. He is obsessed with Haribo. He's always eating it and his car is full of it. There's a woman who lives near him who hands him a packet after every game. So this must have given him – and the team – an extra special bit of gas this time out.

Lee is one of the most underrated players in our squad, someone who never gets the credit he deserves. He's not the quickest but he is the fittest and he's a perfect passer who gets the Saints backs moving very well, while controlling the forwards around the pitch. Lee never lets Northampton down but he just doesn't seem to fit in with what England are looking for, which is unfortunate for him.

Two other of our underrated players, Jon Clarke and Jimmy Downey, followed Lee by coming to the fore in the semi-final against Perpignan. It wasn't the usual stars who got in the spotlight from those two crucial games, which was particularly pleasing.

Perpignan were incredible in their quarter-final in Barcelona, beating Jonny Wilkinson's Toulon, but it was a case of same old, same old with the French. Sometimes they don't travel very well, and luckily for us the semi-final was one of those occasions.

We had to get all those feelings out of our heads in advance of the game, though, as they could have made us over-confident. I've never understood the theory I must admit and clearly one day a French club is going to travel very well and someone is going to get smacked!

In the quarters Ulster matched us in everything we did and played so well, but in the semis Perpignan didn't seem to be the Perpignan we knew and had watched. Their offloading game wasn't there and their huge pack wasn't as dangerous as we've seen in the past. Maybe they had played their Heineken Cup final in the round before, so perhaps anything else would be an anticlimax for them?

Fodes scored early on and from then on the French side just didn't look too interested. We got away from them on the scoreboard with a try just after half-time and they were out of it from then on, as we kicked to the corners and didn't let them back in, winning 23–7.

As I say, this was a day when two of the Northampton guys who rarely get any praise, Jon Clarke and Jimmy Downey, grabbed all the headlines, and I was delighted with that as they're two guys who really do deserve it. They're both players who never seem to get looked at for Test rugby and I'm not sure why. I know Clarkey has had his injury problems, but I'd say he is one of the best 13s in the country. It's the same for Jimmy at 12, who never seems to get any recognition from Ireland. Perhaps it doesn't help Jimmy's cause – or Roger Wilson's for that matter – that he's playing his club rugby outside Ireland. They don't tend to pick players who aren't turning out for the Irish provinces.

However, the Irish boys did get the recognition against Perpignan. Roger is one of our best players every week – he never has a bad game for Northampton, but never gets considered by Ireland. It's unfortunate that has to happen. Bizarrely, Roger was seeing Caprice – yes, that Caprice – during the course of the season. He'd been on a few dates but I'm not sure how serious it was. I think Fodes – who is going out with Una Healy from The Saturdays – set them up together, which I suppose makes sense.

After trying for so long to make the Heineken Cup final, it was a pretty happy dressing room at Milton Keynes that day, as we had finally made it. It had been a bit of a millstone around our necks, so it was great to finally get over the line. One of our key goals that season was to get to the Heineken Cup final and we had made it.

Back in the Aviva Premiership, we went to London Irish in April and I managed to score a try which was later confirmed as the Premiership Try of the Season. This was also the game where Delon Armitage was banned for punching Stephen Myler. I remember seeing Mylo lying there and I didn't know why he was down, but on the bus home after our 26–20 win they showed the incident to us.

Mylo wasn't complaining about it, but I was annoyed with Delon because I wondered why he would do that to a guy who is quiet and doesn't harm anyone. I spoke to Delon about it but he couldn't explain why he did it. My view was that there was no reason for it.

I was delighted that my long-range score against London Irish was named the Try of the Season, although I did think at the time it was because they had run out of people to nominate. There wasn't much to it, just me running it from their half off turnover ball.

We ended the regular season with one of our worst performances, against Leeds Carnegie, just scraping into the semi-finals after beating the side that finished bottom. Leeds were fighting for their lives, though, so I suppose it was understandable that they gave us a tough game.

Yet Leeds were bottom of the table and were relegated. Was it complacency? Even though you do everything to get it out of your head, it's there somewhere. I knew I wasn't going to score too many tries (I did get one) as Fodes completely jinxed the match for me by saying all week that I was going to score a hat-trick. When he was saying that I knew it was never going to happen and I tried telling him this, but he wouldn't listen.

Our run-in ensured we finished fourth in the Aviva Premiership table, which meant a trip to Leicester for the semi-final … a game I and many other people involved will never forget.

9

Manu and the
Heineken Cup Final

Ever been involved in a rugby match that ended in you taking a call from a police sergeant, asking if you'd like to press charges against an opponent? Sounds ludicrous, doesn't it? But that's how Northampton's Aviva Premiership semi-final finished in 2011 after Manu Tuilagi's three-punch combination on me.

The sergeant's call came right out of the blue. Apparently there had been so many complaints made to the police – from people in Leicester – that they were forced to open a file on the incident. The police called the club and the Saints got a message to me, and I took it from there.

I've always made it a rule that I never carry anything on

after the final whistle, which is why I didn't want to get involved in any further action. I quickly decided it was better to put the incident behind me.

There are some people who would have wanted me to take further action after I was hit not once, not twice, but three times in our Premiership semi-final at Leicester.

The first punch barely landed, nor did the second – they were really no more than slaps. But as millions of people watching on television can testify, it was the third punch that was the most shocking. It was a huge right-handed haymaker that landed near my left eye and it caused a massive outcry.

Over the years I've had a number of run-ins with various players (who hasn't?), and although this was the worst of all the incidents down the years, I've always said that once the game is over, the game is over. You should never carry on anything afterwards, a philosophy that was put severely to the test by this incident. Rugby is a physical sport and emotions run high.

I got this from my dad. When I was young he used to often be the touch judge at my matches. If anything happened and I got involved he used to come on the pitch and if I did something I shouldn't have he wouldn't speak to me for days. Those values have stayed with me.

Not surprisingly, I recall the incident with Manu with total clarity. We were getting to them a bit when Manu decided to lose his head eight minutes before half-time. Lee Dickson took a quick tap and often I'm there on his shoulder when he does that. He got tackled and as I was running at the side of him

Manu just took me out off the ball. He smashed me around the chest.

A semi-final between two traditional rivals, in front of 20,000 people, is a massive match, so perhaps the occasion got to him? He took me out and as we got up I pushed him in the back as I would anyone else, not expecting him to get up and do what he did. That just doesn't happen any more. It's not something you expect to happen – for him to get up and throw three punches in my face. It was a shock and I've since had people asking me, 'How did you manage to stand up?'

As soon as it happened I thought he would be sent off. I assumed the officials had seen everything and that justice would be done – which was a red card. 'Good luck, Manu!' I thought. 'There's a red card coming and Leicester will be down to fourteen men.'

I wasn't going to hit him back as I wanted to play the following week. So I got my head taped up and waited for him to be sent off.

Only it didn't happen that way. Referee Wayne Barnes had a long consultation with Robin Goodliffe, the assistant referee nearest to the incident, before taking action. Not only did Manu escape with a yellow card but, to add insult to injury (literally), I was also sin-binned for the incident. Referee Barnes pulled me over and said, 'You're off as well.' I didn't complain, just saw the yellow card and headed for the touch-line. There was nothing I could do.

I had to be taped up as I had two cuts. One occurred after

Manu and the Heineken Cup Final

Dyl (Dylan Hartley) had accidentally kneed me in the face, but that was only a little cut that had been made bigger by the two left-handed punches. It required five stitches.

I remember once being yellow-carded and running off pretty slowly, only to be told that the ten-minute sin-bin didn't start until I was off the field. From that day on, I've always got off as quickly as possible. That's how I want it – I was keen not to delay my sin-bin any longer, and didn't want to waste time arguing.

I also had to have some stitches near my left eye, in the different cut caused by Manu, so when I returned it was with that rather fetching, very large bandage around my head.

After being stitched up I didn't come back out to sit in the sin-bin chair because it was half-time. No one mentioned the incident in the Northampton dressing room during the breather and the furore only started after the match when it became a media storm.

It was only 3–0 to Leicester at half-time so people were more concerned with what we were going to do in the second half. It was obviously a big story in the media, but among the team we had bigger problems to sort out.

I wasn't really bothered about being punched. I was far more bothered about winning the game and crucially at that point we had a sense we could win the game.

Obviously I was furious with what had happened, but I don't think it affected my performance for the rest of the game – but who knows? Perhaps it did without me knowing it.

More relevant as far as I was concerned was that when we emerged for the second half it seemed the wind had changed direction as well. It wasn't going with us but across the pitch and that hurt us. It seemed to be one of those days when things just don't go right for you.

We couldn't get any ball and we couldn't get out of our half. It was very disappointing but that is the way the game went – we just couldn't get a foothold in the game and ended up losing 11–3.

Our defeat was all the more annoying because we felt we could have won this game, and perhaps we would have if the officials had seen the punches and sent Manu off.

Leicester had faltered at home during the season – Saracens had won there and Gloucester drew 41–41 – so we knew they were beatable, but we just couldn't seal the deal. They played well that day but up until that point they had looked vulnerable home and away, so we felt we had a real opportunity.

At the end, all any of the team could think about was that our Premiership season was over. I didn't start to appreciate how big a story I was embroiled in until later.

Manu came over at the end of the game to shake hands. He didn't say sorry, he didn't say anything, he just shook my hand and hugged me. I didn't bear any ill will towards him. All I thought was, 'This is rugby – these things happen. It's a physical sport, just get on with it.' My head was full of disappointment that we had lost and not that I had been punched.

Manu and the Heineken Cup Final

Jim Mallinder was annoyed about the punches and that Manu hadn't been sent off. As he rightly said, how the incident was handled could have changed the outcome. It's obvious that if Manu had been dismissed it would have been a completely different game, because he had been such a key player for them in what was his first full season. But you often don't get the right decisions in a rugby match and this was an example of that.

After the game the rest of the Northampton players were pretty amazed with what had happened, as the repercussions started to sink in and the media made a bigger and bigger deal of it. High-definition TV didn't do anyone any favours as they replayed the incident – frame by frame – over and over again, so it was portrayed as far worse than it actually was.

In the following days it seemed that everyone had an opinion on it and people just wouldn't shut up about it. People were suggesting I should go to the police about it but that was never going to happen, although they did finally come to me.

My mum called to make sure I was okay. That was her only concern and that of my family. They're 100 per cent loyal to me. But like I say, the incident genuinely didn't bother me that much.

What did upset me, however, was the result of the disciplinary hearing. The panel decided to ban Manu for five weeks but also concluded that I had kneed him in the back. I was given the chance to appear at the hearing, but we had the Heineken Cup final that week and I didn't want anything to take my focus away from that.

Splashdown

Although I wasn't there, at the hearing, the club had sent pictures of my eye to the panel, and I thought that the whole case was clear from the television pictures as well.

I wasn't there to put my side of the story, which I know often happens, but I was stunned to hear that I had been accused of kneeing him in the back after he hit me high and before he punched me three times.

Yes, I pushed him in the back, but it was pretty gentle, and he had already floored me with a high tackle, which in some games would have resulted in a penalty or yellow card anyway. To hear my good name dragged through the mud and to discover Manu had his ban reduced from ten weeks to five partly because of my supposed action was very disappointing. I was the innocent party in this incident. I was high-tackled and I was punched three times, yet I'm portrayed as a bad guy in the disciplinary hearing. That is hard to take.

I was wrong to push him, I suppose, but I can categorically say that I did not knee Manu in the back. Once he hit me late and we both went down I went over to him and pushed him, but I can tell you now I did not intentionally or forcefully knee him in the back. So to read that he had got a lighter ban mainly because of that was naturally frustrating for me. I felt that it was ridiculous for me to be accused of that and it's clear to me from the video I didn't do that.

I felt I hadn't done anything wrong. I thought I'd handled the whole incident quite well, as well as I could have in fact. So you can imagine how disappointed I was to hear that the conclusion of the disciplinary panel was that I'd provoked him. To me it was absolute nonsense, and I was frustrated.

I don't regret staying away from the hearing because it was set for a date so close to the Heineken Cup final – it just wasn't an option as I saw it. It's not really for me to judge whether the length of Manu's suspension fitted the crime – that is the job of the disciplinary committee. What do you give someone who is young and hasn't done anything before?

But the big consequence for Manu was that he missed the Aviva Premiership final – which would have been the biggest game of his life – and the Churchill Cup.

When it first happened I was also a little annoyed that Manu didn't contact me, whether by phone or text, to apologise, although as the weeks went on those feelings disappeared. I got over any disappointment about that quickly.

These sorts of things happen in sport – you see it all the time in football when a bad tackle goes in. But if I ever lost my head in a similar way and lashed out at a fellow player, I like to think I'd apologise to them. Even if it's just the player's agent you're contacting, you should try to get hold of someone.

I didn't talk to Martin Johnson about it, but Brian Smith did send me a text soon afterwards saying, 'Well done for staying on your feet.'

I had to put the whole Manu thing aside at the time for the Heineken Cup final, and perhaps that helped me deal with it. I had to take it out of my mind as we had such a big game.

I'd had some incredible things happen to me in rugby union

over the twelve months before the Manu Tuilagi incident, most of them good, and this extraordinary 2010–11 season ended with another unforgettable match: the Heineken Cup final.

We had been one of the few teams in the history of the competition to go through the pool stage unbeaten, eventually finding ourselves in an epic final at the Millennium Stadium against Brian O'Driscoll's Leinster.

We went into the game as massive underdogs, something we didn't mind. We also heard that some of the bookmakers had paid out for a Leinster win before the game kicked off, which we thought was pretty strange. How you can do that is beyond me.

We were pretty happy with our preparation and state of mind, and that showed in the first half when we produced almost the perfect forty minutes, powering into a 22–6 lead.

We had been trying for so long, since the turn of the century, to make the Heineken Cup final and the day itself was massive for the club.

The whole focus from Jim and the coaches was to make this game as normal as any other. We travelled down to Cardiff the day before and everything was normal. No one seemed to be too nervous and I for one had a great feeling about the day, which translated into our first-half performance. Everyone was ready, everyone knew it would be our last game of the season, so we would have no excuse for not using up every ounce of our efforts in taking the famous trophy back to Northampton.

We were missing Tom Wood as he tried everything he could to recover from a broken leg. He even tried to complete a training session in the week of the final to prove his fitness, but he was running around like a pirate on one leg so we all just said 'Woody, get off!' and he had to accept the inevitable.

Even when Jim came round with his piece of paper to read out the team on the Wednesday before the game, Tom shouted 'Am I in, Jim?' and everyone laughed at him. There was never any chance he could make it.

The final itself started a bit strangely. We had been starting games poorly all year but in this match we didn't put a foot wrong in those opening exchanges. Early on I remember saying to Fodes (Ben Foden), 'How good is this?' We were pushing them off every single ball – which doesn't happen – and we scored three tries in a matter of thirty minutes through Phil Dowson, Fodes and Dyl. It was the perfect start and we began to believe we could do it.

But it did feel strange that we were so far ahead, and in a final against the favourites and 2009 champions too. We went in at half-time sixteen points up and it had a surreal feel about it.

All the coaches could really say at half-time was 'Keep it going' because it was the perfect half of rugby. It was a dream for it to go so easily. And I think now because it went so easily that it didn't help us get into the game in the second half, because we expected to do the same again. The second half was the complete opposite, and we weren't ready for that.

I remember running out for the second half and when I

came down the tunnel I could see Leinster were already out there, ready to kick off. They were ready to go.

Dyl had received a big bang to his head when he scored his try and – in hindsight – he should really have come off. At half-time he didn't say much. It was a bigger hit than people realised and we later discovered he actually had concussion. I think Dyl often pulls the other two front-rowers, Soane Tonga'uiha and Brian Mujati, with him, so when he was affected by his head knock, strangely so were they. To lose Dyl in the second half was a big blow to our momentum. We lost a couple of scrums and you could almost feel the sense of belief surge back into Leinster. They thought the tide had turned.

And they were right. We started going backwards and what had been a dream performance turned into a nightmare.

I did get one chance in the second half and it almost ended in me getting a serious injury as I was smashed from the side at the end of my run. The pain in my shin was initially pretty bad and in the investigations afterwards it was discovered that I'd been playing with a stress fracture of the shin. We aren't sure how long it had been there, but it took this hit to find it.

I know people said we ran out of steam. I know Soane was tired because I spoke to him afterwards. Normally when you get ahead 22–6 the second half is quite easy. But this time we couldn't kick the corners and play the percentages, we just couldn't get the ball off them. No matter what we did, we couldn't get it off them and they were making breaks all over the pitch. I think the lads just blew up and the wheels came off all over the pitch.

People were blown away. I didn't feel it slipping away immediately, but when Johnny Sexton scored his and Leinster's second try about ten minutes into the half I feared the worst. Things just weren't happening for us and crucially we just couldn't get the ball to relieve the pressure. That was such an unusual position for us to be in, especially in the Heineken Cup when we had won every match up until this point.

People's heads began to drop and that is such a bad thing. Perhaps it was because we hadn't been in a similar situation before. It does happen to people in sport – their heads just go and it's so hard to turn it round. We just self-combusted.

I don't know whether Ireland's Six Nations win over England a couple of months previously was relevant, whether that gave them the confidence to believe they could come back from such a deficit.

That certainly wasn't in my mind. You could argue that some of the Saints players could draw strength from playing at the Millennium Stadium. When we were last there as England players we enjoyed a magnificent win against Wales, so that should have given us confidence. We had that on our side but it didn't matter.

For me it's tough when the team is going backwards and you're relying on other people to help you out. It slipped away and when Leinster came back they were like an unstoppable force. I'm not sure if that suggests a flaw in our side that we need to address. Hopefully there's not a lack of belief deep down.

One guy who didn't take a backward step was Courtney Lawes. He just loves tackling and put his body on the line time and time again. He played like a fourth back-rower.

I think he's only just realised how big he is. He's started to become himself now. Courtney just loves hitting people and he loves tackling. England have timed it just right and brought him into the team slowly. That has made him more hungry, more desperate to play.

Courtney has the potential to be something a bit special on the world stage. His levels of desire are huge. His rise is remarkable because when I arrived at the club he looked to be a player without the desire. It seemed to me that he didn't want to train. He had no interest at all.

I remember standing at the bottom of the hill for one of our pre-season training sessions and there was Courtney. He just wouldn't do it and Nick Johnston, our performance director, was shouting his head off at him, while Courtney wasn't listening.

He used to train with this massive cream hoodie on under his T-shirt. I thought he was a lad from the academy who couldn't be bothered, but look at him now. He's completely changed and is one of the most enthusiastic trainers you'll ever see.

Courtney has been outstanding for Northampton, and his rise is testament to Jim and Nobby (Dorian West) as I think he could have drifted away. They obviously had huge faith in him right from the start.

A few times we've been out with the lads and sometimes we'll come across one of those punching machines. We're all there hitting it as hard as we can, getting okay scores, and then Courtney strolls up and almost breaks the thing. His brother is thirteen, and almost as big as him, but he thinks he's going to play basketball.

Even with the positives, we were very down after losing to Leinster. But we shouldn't see the 2010–11 season as a failure because we reached a Heineken Cup final and Aviva Premiership semi-final. And I'm glad Jim's reaction wasn't to dismantle the team. He made some new signings in the summer that followed but most were to cover the number of players who would be away at the World Cup in September and October.

After the game we all sat in the dressing room in silence. We knew Leinster were a good team and capable of making a comeback, but the main feeling was disbelief. We couldn't get over what had happened. How did we concede 27 points in one half?

It was such a shame to see our season end that way but you learn from games and experiences like that, and what happened in Cardiff on 21 May 2011 will stand us in good stead. When we're in that position next time we'll be better for it. Slowly but surely we're getting there.

It's awful when you're in the middle of it, but few people

remember the times Leinster just failed. All people remember is them winning the Heineken Cup in 2009 and 2011, but they had some agonising defeats along the way too.

That night I just kept myself with the lads and got a few drinks inside me. But Jim and the coaches made a good decision to come with us for once. They usually – quite rightly – keep their distance from our nights out but it was important we all drowned our sorrows together on this occasion.

Everyone had given everything they had but we were still bitterly disappointed, although no one could criticise the lads for lack of effort. We didn't have any more to give. Jim was upset about it and like us he couldn't believe what had happened – we had one hand on the Heineken Cup.

Northampton may not have reached the Aviva Premiership final, but I still got to go because I made my debut as a TV pundit. And I enjoyed my day looking on at Twickenham.

The final came a couple of days after my knee operation, so I was still on crutches and not allowed to stand for too long. So to get me into the commentary box area, ESPN laid on a wheelchair, which I didn't really need but it made good TV.

I enjoyed my first time on the box but I'm not sure anyone heard much of what I said because all the Leicester fans sang 'Manu, Manu, Manu' every time I spoke. Fans outside in the car park surrounded the commentary box so I took a lot of good-humoured stick. It was only a couple of weeks since Manu had punched me so I still had the scars to prove it.

I was joined by Minty (Nick Easter), who looked like Harry Hill from *TV Burp*. He turned up with a jacket and a shirt with a massive collar outside of his blazer, which I think had stains on it as well. Unfortunately he wasn't as funny as Harry Hill but that's what you get with Minty.

I think ESPN have added quite a lot to the game since covering matches live and I thought I did okay. I didn't do too much preparation, but friends and family got in touch afterwards and confirmed that at least I didn't swear!

Even though they've been our rivals for a while I was delighted that Saracens won it. They really did deserve it on the day – holding out the Tigers heroically in the last few minutes – and I was really pleased because I'm sick of Leicester winning it every year!

It was a really good day of sport for me, as from the Premiership final I was whisked off to the Champions League final at Wembley. I'm not a Manchester United fan as such, but I suppose if I supported any football team it would be United. I was delighted to see them play a wonderful Barcelona side, who in winning showed themselves to be one of the greatest teams ever to play the game.

10

Under the Knife

I endured a frustrating start to England's World Cup training camp, which began at the start of June. I was delighted to be named in the forty-five-man squad, but I knew I'd start behind everyone else as I needed a long-overdue knee operation.

I had a number of dates pencilled in for the operation, but once we lost the Aviva Premiership semi-final at Leicester I knew it would come within forty-eight hours of the Heineken Cup final.

The surgeons took half the cartilage out from the inside of my left knee. It had torn and the bones were badly bruised because of playing on it for the season. My knee was spot on for the start of the World Cup, although the docs told me there's a chance I'll get arthritis in it when I'm older.

That isn't something I feel too bad about at the moment though!

I had no real choice but to have the operation that had left me on the sidelines in those early weeks of the camp. My knee was sore for most of the season, and when I scored my tries against Australia last November I was already injured. But players carry on with injuries like this all the time. Am I ever 100 per cent fit? I doubt it, and it's the same with most professional players. Maybe after pre-season you're fit, but once the season starts everyone picks up niggles; but you don't want to miss a game for club or country.

No club or your country would ever force you to play with an injury. I can only speak for myself but I push it myself, more than any medic I've ever come across, as all they want is the best for you. I get wonderful care at both Northampton and England and I'm twisting their arms to be allowed to play, not the other way round.

In my case there is a little bit of cartilage left, but not as much as you should have in a normal knee. I picked up the injury early in the season playing for Northampton, so could have stopped at any time to have the operation, although I decided pretty quickly I wasn't going to let it disrupt my season, and it could wait until the end of the campaign. Unless I can't run I won't miss a game and the final weeks of any season are so important, a time you don't want to miss any games.

As part of my recovery from my knee operation, I was able

to get away on holiday with Melissa to Mauritius. Since being at Northampton I've become quite friendly with former England Test cricketer Allan Lamb, who is a big Saints fan, so he helped arrange a trip to the Sugar Beach Resort on the island. A few of the South African lads at Northampton knew Allan and the holiday was arranged through his travel company.

We went out there for ten days. I just wanted a holiday where I could relax and do nothing. I was still recovering from my operation so had treatment every day with a portable ice machine that the club had given me to take away. It was a season when so much had happened. The year before had been incredible, with me ending up as the Premiership's Player of the Season, so at the time I didn't think things could get much better and more hectic. But as things turned out I was wrong about that, and a holiday away from everything was just what I needed to recharge the batteries.

It was the perfect trip because my body was tired. It had taken a battering through the season, more so than usual, so I stuck to the plan of taking it easy. I wasn't able to go the extra step and switch off my phone while I was on the island though – there was too much going on at home for that. I did lock it away during the day but felt compelled to check it when we went back to the room. Melissa understands and it seems that I ended up giving her more stick for being on the phone than me!

With the World Cup just around the corner, I was under

doctor's orders to go easy, and that wasn't difficult on a ten-day tropical island break. We quickly got into a relaxing routine: each day we'd wake up to the glorious sight of the Indian Ocean before having breakfast and lounging under a palm tree by the pool. I swam a few laps every day to help with my rehab before stretching out on the white-sand beach, which was a few feet from our front door.

It wasn't all sitting on my backside, though, as I would often grab a snorkel and mask and wade into the turquoise water. And I didn't completely switch off, because I worked a few weights at the gym to keep up the fitness.

One night there was a lunar eclipse. I had no idea it was going to happen when we flew out, and couldn't believe it when people at the hotel told us. We stayed up to watch it. It was amazing, the sky was so clear. I don't think you could ever get anything like that in Britain.

And while we were there we met people from the Mauritius Rugby Union – the director of rugby, the president of the union, and a player who had met Ben Cohen and Jonny Wilkinson when they had visited the island. Only 800 people play rugby in Mauritius so they explained how hard they were working to make the game grow. Only a few years ago they had barely 200 players, so things are moving in the right direction.

The day we were leaving coincided with Mauritius playing against the French island of Réunion, so we went along on the way to the airport. And when I got there they asked me to kick off the match, which I did. It was the first time in my career that I've taken a kick-off! I made sure I did it with my right leg, so I was okay.

The last time I even took a kick in a rugby match was when Northampton were in Division 1, although I used to do quite a bit of goal-kicking for Wigan. It was pretty surreal to be there on Mauritius kicking off a game.

Seeing how much the game meant to the players before the game, singing their anthem, made a big impression on me. Their level of commitment didn't seem any less than that of the England squad. I stood right in front of them and watched them sing the anthems and it was great to see how much it meant to them. The team consisted of a lot of players of French origin while in the crowd there were a lot of South Africans, making it a pretty cosmopolitan occasion.

As always, there were a few rugby fans around the island and, although I'm not the most high-profile player, I did get recognised a few times, especially by Welsh people. They gave me some stick but I always had the comeback of our win in Cardiff a few months before.

Arriving back from Mauritius, my knee still wasn't right, which I hadn't expected. I kept getting some pain, which started to worry me a little. It was a shooting pain that affected me when I walked, and came back when I started training.

The physios weren't worried, however, and told me that as I built up the muscles around my knee the pain would go away. I was a bit annoyed because I'd gone to the trouble of having the operation and I'd expected it to clear up the problem, but I suppose life is rarely as simple as that.

It was preying on my mind a little as I got ready to start the most important part of my life in rugby union: the build-up to the 2011 Rugby World Cup. The time for talking (and going on holidays) was over.

I hate missing even one training session, so when the squad got together at Pennyhill Park in Bagshot it killed me to stand on the sidelines watching them. I knew full well it was for my benefit in the long run, but that didn't help my level of frustration. All I wanted to do was get out there and play so that I could help guarantee my spot for the World Cup.

The strange thing was there wasn't much fanfare, if any. The squad wasn't announced but as I was in the England Elite Player squad of thirty-two, I was told to turn up at Pennyhill Park. When I got there it was confirmed that it was us plus thirteen other players who would make up the initial World Cup squad.

I had been speaking to England's attack coach Brian Smith, but there was no official letter or phone call telling me I had made the squad. After the Heineken Cup final, Smithy texted me a message saying 'hard luck' and saying he would see me in a few weeks, which I suppose is the closest to announcing it to me. Of course I hope that if I hadn't made it someone would have told me, rather than let me just turn up!

Most teams have a camp like ours, which started the three-month run-in to New Zealand. And my fears about missing the World Cup were heightened by the way Martin Johnson laid down the law when we arrived in Bagshot. We had barely got through the door of the hotel when we were called into a team meeting during which he left us in no doubt – if any remained – that none of us were guaranteed a place at the World Cup. 'If you don't pay attention, if you don't switch on now,' Johnno told us, 'then you will fall between the cracks, and someone else will take your place. If you aren't ready to work hard, you should go and get a taxi now.'

Of course the lads were using this in every training session, taking the mick. If anyone did anything wrong someone was guaranteed to say, 'You're falling through the cracks' or 'Go and get a taxi!'

Johnno meant every word of it and each of us knew – in all seriousness – that if we dropped off at training we'd be on our way home. Why would anyone who knows Martin Johnson think he was joking!

I regarded it as a massive honour to be involved in my first World Cup squad, even if this squad had forty-five players in it and only thirty would go to New Zealand. I was glad to be there and to be in the room with the rest of the lads. I didn't know exactly who had and hadn't made it beforehand, so when I walked into that meeting I was fascinated to see who was there.

My first reaction was 'Wow, there are a lot of players in this room.' More than I'd ever seen before, in fact. It's good to have new faces around the squad and a lot of them were really young. Johnno had called up seven wingers, which I thought was unusual, so in my position the competition was, and is, very high.

It made me appreciate what healthy competition there was for the wing spots in the England squad, but we all knew Johnno wouldn't be taking more than three wings to New Zealand so it also increased my usual levels of anxiety. It was pretty clear none of us were yet booked on the plane to the World Cup.

Wing hasn't been a strong area for England for a while so it's good to see there are a lot of wingers and a lot of good players coming through . . . good news for Johnno. The seven wingers in the room were myself, Matt Banahan, Mark Cueto, Charlie Sharples, David Strettle, James Simpson-Daniel and Ugo Monye. A few of those, like Banahan and Simpson-Daniel, can play other positions of course, but it's still competition for me. Also in the squad was Delon Armitage, a full-back who can also play wing – as we were to see at the World Cup.

We all knew that a third of the squad would be sent home by the middle of August so it was a competitive environment for sure.

And as I say, if anyone in the room did believe they had made it, Johnno rocked that theory with his first address to the squad. He said that whether players had been in the squad for ten minutes or ten years it didn't matter and that every single person in the room had an equal chance of making it.

Johnno spelled out how much hard work was ahead before

we got to the first game against Wales on 6 August and before the squad for New Zealand was announced sixteen days later.

As usual I was sharing a room with Ben Foden. I'm always with Fodes so when I turned up at the hotel I didn't even need to ask. It was even the same room as we shared during the Six Nations. We were bored with the first one so we asked to change and they put us in one which is exactly the same but reversed! Some of the rooms at Pennyhill have a mezzanine floor inside them, but Fodes and I don't get anywhere near them. I think you need more than fifty caps to be allocated one of those.

I just wanted to get my head down on this training camp and work hard. I regarded it as a massive honour to be involved. It was my first World Cup so I wanted to make a good impression. Fodes normally arrives at an 8pm meeting at 7.59 and 30 seconds. I used to push the timings too but I kept being late.

Manu Tuilagi was in the room, which was the first time I knew he had made the squad. Hardly surprising after such a great season for him but it was clear I might have had an issue to settle with him after what had happened the last time we met!

I wanted him to be there as I think he's a great player and one who can add a lot to England. You want those kinds of people in the squad – he'd had a great season and had been the best number 13 in England without a doubt.

It wasn't something I was thinking about before we met up because it was water under the bridge to a certain extent, but

Under the Knife

I didn't want there to be an atmosphere between us as I hope we'll be playing together for England for many years to come.

I was waiting for my chance to meet him, although none of the coaches or management mentioned it to me. If anything it was a joking point among some of the other players – certainly Richard Wigglesworth and Danny Care were winding me up to speak to him. I also got a bit of stick from being on Twitter saying I would be meeting up with Manu again, but nothing much more. You take it all with a pinch of salt.

During my rugby league days, there were stories that certain players couldn't be in the same room together or they would fight all the time. However, that certainly wasn't the case between Manu and me.

So in that first team meeting I went up to him, shook his hand and made it clear we were starting with a clean sheet of paper. 'I haven't seen you since you tried to take my head off my shoulders,' I said and he just laughed – he did this little chuckle. All the lads were laughing at this. 'Tell me what you were thinking,' I asked him and he just laughed again. He came and sat down with us and asked how my knee was and that was it. From getting to know him a bit since, it's clear he's a really nice lad.

Speaking to some of the Leicester lads, it was obvious he just wanted to forget about it and get on with things, which was fine by me. I don't mind. We had a bit of a laugh with the lads and when I spoke to him in the following weeks he always made a big effort to ask how I was.

Splashdown

We may not ever be the greatest of friends (not because he punched me three times in a club match), but what is clear to me is that we're team-mates intent on achieving the most we can in an England shirt. The bottom line is that Manu is a great player who I believe can contribute a huge amount to the England cause, so I was delighted to have him alongside me. What happened between us happened and it was now time to put it behind us – I know Manu felt the same and being with him in the England squad made this easier. We're past the incident now and I can talk about normal things with him.

My injury meant I was on the sidelines in one sense, but that concept doesn't really exist with England when you're at a training camp, so instead of getting out on the pitch I was confined to the marquee that had been erected at the hotel for our fitness work.

Being injured doesn't mean you sit in your room watching TV, because England have a plan for every single player. Mine involved stepping into what I can only describe as a torture chamber that Johnno had erected in the grounds of the hotel. At one of the most luxurious hotels in Britain, with a wonderful spa and swimming pool, I was being flogged on a number of machines in the marquee.

They have all these horrible machines specially adapted for us – specially adapted to put us through pain more like! They had rowers, skiing machines, weightless running machines and spinning bikes – you name any machine and it was there – mind, they were modified so that they didn't put pressure on my knee. The fitness staff with England seemed to have transformed all these machines into rowing machines, but ones that tested different parts of your body.

The worst one is the Wattbike, which is a spinning bike with a rowing wheel stuck on. There was another machine, which was a skier, a SkiErg, for shoulders, backs and legs – again, it's nothing you'd see in a normal gym.

One I found very useful was an AlterG, which allowed me to use a treadmill weightlessly. It can take all your bodyweight and you feel almost the same benefit that you would on a normal treadmill – it still made me tired anyway. As it was so light on my feet, I felt I could run forever on that machine.

During the early part of the camp the boys were doing three rotations of speed and skills, weights and resting. That's forty minutes each and quite hard work, and while they were doing that I'd watch the wrestling, as they were trying to learn pretty technical skills for rucking and tackling. I'd do rehab while they were doing their speed work.

The coaches also put in a number of team challenges for these machines once or twice a week. They split us into teams of six to see who could travel the furthest in six minutes. For example, I would hit it hard for twenty seconds and then make way for another team member. Because of my injury I didn't do it in week one and my team won. However, when I joined them for week two we came last, so you know who they all blamed.

I'd love to meet the guy who invented these machines, as he

needs a good talking-to. The Wattbike and the SkiErg are the worst without doubt. If you're injured with England it's no reason to sit in your room all day, that's for sure. The fitness team can always think of something to do, no matter what. It was intense work, but that's what you need if you're going to play for your country, and going to go to a World Cup – deep down as players we wouldn't have it any other way.

There are no questions asked and if there are, well . . . you can order yourself a taxi!

In the afternoon the players often did a long rugby session but before the day really got going the staff ran a Fat Club, where we had this 'get up and go' group. You don't eat different food in there but take part in different activities. And while I know you want some names I can't reveal the identities of those in the Fat Club. My lips are sealed. Although I can reveal I put myself in there at one point as I'd had a bit too much to eat. Those not in the Fat Club might fit into another of the specialist groups. There is a Shoulder Group or a Glutes Club.

One of the main activities for the Fat Club is a bike ride in the countryside around Bagshot and I thought that would do my knee some good. It was good getting out there in the morning to start the day, even if it brought some stick from scrum coach Wig (Graham Rowntree), who often led the rides. Wig seems to think that as I'm a Northerner I should have a whippet to come out with me on my bike rides. He also thinks I can communicate with the dogs so if any chased after us it was down to me to talk to them and get rid of them.

The team was also asked to take part in 'protected sleep' – when the management insist we get our heads down during the day – but I struggled to do that as I can't sleep in the day.

At the start of the camp I was pretty much the only one in the marquee, getting flogged. There I was on those machines looking out at the lads playing rugby in the sun. It was hard to take but I knew I was heading in the right direction and going through the agony to get myself in the shape needed to go to a World Cup.

The one thing I did manage to avoid was the set of wrestling sessions that conditioner Paul Stridgeon had put together. In busy Test weeks we would never be able to fit in a session like wrestling, but being together for so long gave Paul the chance to introduce what is a useful skill into our training.

We started doing King of the Ring at the end of the session, which involved people being pushed out of the ring. That got very competitive and usually saw either Banners (Matt Banahan) or Manu left at the end. You have to leave them to the end so they can fight it out between themselves.

It can get quite tasty as the competitive spirit takes over. It was full on and it wasn't long before we had picked up our first injury as Ben Youngs went down with his knee after one session. You can't expect to have the squad wrestling and not pick up some injuries, but I think there was already a problem there anyway, so at least this made him finally get it sorted.

You can't temper how hard you go at these events. What is

the difference between rugby and wrestling? You're just as likely to get injured in a rugby session as you are while wrestling. You can't not train as you're going to play and you can't train trying to avoid injuries. It just doesn't work that way. My attitude with something like wrestling would always be to go full on, especially as there are coaches on the sidelines shouting. You wouldn't expect any less.

With England we do a number of measurable training sessions, especially now that we're using GPS technology in training, the packs sitting in a vest we wear under our shirts. We will run forty metres and Stretts (David Strettle) was the fastest the last time we did it in the Six Nations. He did it in 5.3 seconds, and I wasn't far behind that. Once when I did one my shins were too sore for me to carry on. I get bad shins as well, especially when the ground is hard.

England have used Dutch speed coach Frans Bosch, who I enjoyed working with, but on the whole I don't like sprint coaches as they try to change my running style.

But Frans was different. He left your running style as it was and tried to add in his own techniques. But during the season he started working with Wales, so unfortunately he wasn't with England when we went to the World Cup.

I used to do quite a lot of road running, and still like to now. I always liked to run and from an early age used to go out with my dad. He'd do around four miles every morning, and because he did so much running and played so much rugby his knee went as well.

Under the Knife

I used to go with him and at first I used to be miles behind, ending up crying, stuck in the trees. But then as I got older I ended up ahead of him. I always enjoyed it so I carried on, but I might not be able to do as much of that now, or for as long. It might be good enough for me, mentally and fitness-wise, but it won't be good for my knee any more.

Within the England set-up Johnno is constantly talking with the physios, getting the full picture of every player's injuries, so we all know if I'm going to miss a match or training session. I think they have meetings every night when we're with England so Johnno gets a daily bulletin on the status of every player with a report on whether he can train or play.

Strangely, during the year my knee was most painful when I was walking, rather than sprinting, which I thought was odd. I have absolutely no idea why that was. Perhaps it made me want to run faster? I ended up unable to do things like go shopping in a supermarket because I would just be limping around.

But if it came to running I was pretty much okay, and as that is a big part of my job I was relieved. I don't know what it was and no one ever explained it to me. It wasn't a problem at the start of the season, but I kept catching it in training and the knee would lock, and click it out. That kept happening even more regularly, giving me some sharp pain, but luckily the pain would go quite quickly.

I noticed my left leg was starting to become thinner and thinner as the season went on as I was using my right leg more to compensate. I really noticed it at the end of the season, when we played in the Heineken Cup final. My knee wasn't working properly so the muscles weren't firing properly.

In the last few weeks of the season I was really struggling walking around. Stopping was hard work but running was fine and I don't know if that was because I was overusing my right leg, and obviously in games adrenalin was kicking in. I had it strapped up in every game but in the Heineken Cup final, which was a bit of a disaster all round, I managed to get another injury.

In the course of my career I've been lucky but I suppose that may have something to do with the fact that I'm only twenty-four. Injuries tend to start coming on a more regular basis when a player hits twenty-eight and beyond.

Injuries are part of the life of a professional rugby player. If you take on a contact sport like rugby you will get injured, and the reality of that has never bothered me. You take the rough with the smooth, and I was lucky enough that the knee injury didn't lead to me missing any games in the season. I'm not one for missing games. Even the week my dad died, in May 2010, I didn't miss the game afterwards. My dad, who was an engineer and a teacher, was the sort of man who never missed a day's work, so that ethic runs in the family.

11

Starting to Get Serious

The months of June and July seemed to flash by and before I knew it we were again sitting in the team room at Pennyhill Park, hearing the names of the team to take on Wales in our first World Cup warm-up game at Twickenham.

In the team meeting we had been going over moves, watching games and getting used to being back playing Test matches with England. We were given a playbook for all moves at the start of the training camp in June, but that changed for the week of the first Wales game in August, as it would for almost every match.

The World Cup may have been on the horizon but you have to focus on what's right in front of you. In this case it was Wales, even if it was billed as a warm-up. As far as I'm concerned – and I know the other players feel the same – a Test match is a Test match. It's another precious chance to pull on that England jersey and, who knows, score another try for your country.

We were also left in no doubt that if we got it wrong in that first match there might be no World Cup for some of us. It would be daft to look towards a game in September when you have three games to play in August. At the time I wouldn't have been arrogant enough to assume I was in the World Cup squad anyway, so the next game is always the important one for me. It's obvious that the management was looking towards the World Cup and planning ahead, but you can't afford to do that as a player.

I really enjoyed the camp, even if I couldn't take a full part in all of it, because it was a chance to spend time and train with the best players in the country and to continue developing my game. That's another thing Johnno said to us – that every player should take the chance in the training camp to develop themselves as a player.

There was a lot going on in terms of commercial offers off the field as well but I was conscious not to do too much in that area. We get commercial offers all the time but in a World Cup year it's crucial to pick and choose the right ones.

I was asked to go on a rugby version of *Come Dine with Me* (called *Scrum Dine with Me*). That wasn't something I wanted to do, but I did do an advert for the England team sponsor, O2, with Martin Johnson and a number of the other England players. You have to make a judgement call, I suppose, and I thought it was far more acceptable to do something that was being done by quite a few members of the team, rather than something on my own. Doing an advert was something completely new for me and it was good fun filming it.

I think the England management judge it quite well and the players realise we can't be doing loads of stuff. They're trying to help us in that respect. Everyone wants Jonny Wilkinson at every event, but these opportunities all get shared out among the team.

The advert involved us going to someone's house, waking them up and taking them downstairs to make them an O2 breakfast pie. Then they went into the living room where Johnno was waiting with a remote control to watch an England match, as all the games were broadcast early in the morning in the UK.

The attitude to training from everyone was that every session was precious. We might have been together for a number of weeks but we needed to wring every last drop out of every session – they were all that important. You could tell everyone was switched on for the fitness sessions and the training. Everyone was desperate to beat everyone else, and it would be odd if that hadn't been the case because we were gearing up for a World Cup with forty-five players in the squad, knowing that only thirty would be getting on the plane to New Zealand.

All the fitness scores are top secret outside the squad, but they're all put up for all the players to see, which raises the competition. Everything is up there on the walls – including body fat – so you can't hide.

To begin with the focus was on the fitness side but by the end of July, as the Wales game came into view, it turned to rugby. The message was that everyone was equal and Johnno made sure everyone was well aware there was no number one in certain positions. We all had to fight to make the thirty.

All forty-five players were given World Cup contracts but I didn't read mine. If I have to sign a bit of paper to play in a World Cup I will sign it. If you don't sign it you won't be able to play in the World Cup, so that doesn't give you too many options. And also I trust the people, the RPA (Rugby Players' Association) who negotiate these contracts on our behalf.

They also have the GPS contract, which you need to sign to allow people who you play against or are in your team to wear a GPS unit during a match. I'm more than happy to wear the units, which are like small mobile phones in vests, in training but I didn't want to wear them in a match. England are fine with people making their own decisions on this.

There was no block on us using social media like Twitter and Facebook. Johnno's opinion is that we're old enough to make our own decisions and are able to decide what to put and what not to put in those places. Some of the older players hate it and ask why the lads are on Twitter, while I know New Zealand put a complete ban on their players using it, because it can cause trouble. You don't think sometimes and you can put something on Twitter which you believe won't offend anyone but which turns out to do exactly that.

My view is that if people want to do it they should be allowed. Just because you join a rugby team it shouldn't prevent you from communicating with fans on Twitter. I recently broke into Fodes' Twitter account when he left his phone switched on and I sent a message to his girlfriend Una and posted a message saying he hated everyone who wasn't as good-looking as he was.

He told me later he got loads of offensive messages back from people who thought he was serious, calling him arrogant. Other people sent me messages straightaway because they figured out what had happened. Fodes only realised a few hours later when Una called him up and he wasn't happy, so I knew to be on my guard!

In terms of training we went straight into playing rugby. Not much contact but working on moves, drills and match scenarios.

It was quite an intense period for me as I went from playing in a Heineken Cup final to having a short holiday to starting my pre-season in June. But that's what happens if you want to play rugby for your country and go to a World Cup. It's part of what you need to go through, so you get on with it and thank your lucky stars you're there, rather than on a longer holiday or in that taxi Johnno talked about.

The weeks in that summer period were heavy but as a rule we ended them on either Thursday or Friday, so you were able to go home at the weekends, something that helped keep us fresh. That small amount of free time allowed me to go to a number of events that I hadn't been able to attend before: the Glastonbury Festival in Somerset and the tennis at Wimbledon. I'd wanted to go to Glastonbury for a number of years and this summer the chance came around through a couple of friends who always go to festivals and are heavily involved in it.

Melissa wanted to go but as the invite was for myself and Dyl we decided to go by ourselves on the Friday (U2 night) and stay overnight. We had a great time. We were lucky enough to get a helicopter into the grounds, which made arriving a lot easier, but we couldn't avoid the rain, which poured down from the moment we landed. The mud was about two foot deep, which wasn't great for my knee or for Dyl's back.

Glastonbury is an amazing place, like a little town. A friend has a Winnebago so we spent some time in that and we actually ended up staying in a luxury tent. Even so, we kept getting wet and because we hadn't brought too many clothes the only way we could think of keeping dry was to use the various fancy-dress stalls they have at Glastonbury.

That would have been fine in itself but towards the end of the night, when I was dressed as a firefighter and Dyl as a monk, we wandered into one of the tents to watch a band. It was hot in there so I undid my top, only to find myself getting more and more attention from the (mostly) men inside. After being in there a few minutes it suddenly dawned on me that

My knee injury was playing on my mind as I got ready to start the most important part of my life in rugby union: the build-up to the Rugby World Cup. Here I am trying to get fit at Pennyhill Park.

Despite not being fit for the Wales warm-up games, I was delighted when I got the call from Johnno to say that I'd made the squad. Here I am with the boys preparing for the Ireland game.

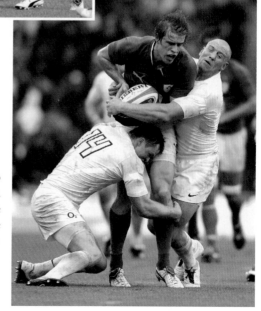

We couldn't wait to get back to Dublin to avenge the Six Nations defeat. Even though Ireland never got a foothold in the match it was a frustrating game for me personally.

We touched down in NZ and it immediately hit me that I had arrived in more ways than one – it struck me how lucky I was to have made it.

England v Argentina, 10 September 2011: Crucially we made a winning start to the world cup, though we had to really work for it, finally winning 13–9.

England v Georgia, 18 September 2011: The Georgia game was tough but we ended up winning 41–10 and I was chuffed to score two tries.

England v Romania, 24 September 2011: We went into the Romania game in good spirits and we scored a lot of tries! This is my first of a hat-trick . . .

My second try . . .

. . . and my third.

England v Scotland, 1 October 2011: We confirmed our place in the quarter-finals after beating Scotland 16–12, staying unbeaten in the pool with only one try conceded.

My try took me to the top of the tournament try-scoring charts with six, but none of that mattered when we entered the knockout stage against France . . .

England v France, 8 October 2011: There was no point in the game when I didn't feel we could take them so we were incredibly frustrated to concede such a bad try when Vincent Clerc scored.

Going out of the World Cup at the quarter-final stage was the most gut-wrenching feeling of my career. I was devastated by our exit, it's as simple as that.

We were lucky to be able to experience some of the amazing adventure sports New Zealand has to offer on our days off. White-water rafting was great fun.

I'd never done a bungy jump before but I ended up addicted, doing it four times!

Some down time with the boys in a restaurant in Auckland. From left to right: Dyl, Joe Simpson, Alex Corbisiero, me and my manager Rob Burgess.

'm very lucky to have a loving and supportive family. Here I am with my brother David, Mum nd sisters Beth and Claire.

With my far better other half,
Melissa, at Tins and Zara's wedding.

With my dad and David in Paris for my first England game – the only one my dad got to see of me in an England shirt. I'm so glad all my family were there.

One man who's been right beside me through the highs and lows – my dad, Kevin Ashton. What I've learnt from the passing of my dad is that life is never straightforward. I always thought it was.

this was a gay event, and I was standing there looking like a reject from the Village People. Hilarious!

After Glastonbury it was back into training but I was lucky enough to get an invitation to the tennis at Wimbledon and the women's singles final. Everyone grows up watching the tennis at Wimbledon but I'd never had the chance to go before, so when Nike's Barney Keeler offered me the chance to go I snapped his hand off.

It also gave me the chance to make up for not taking Melissa to Glastonbury as I could take her to Wimbledon. She loved it too, as it was a pretty glamorous event.

When I was growing up, the tennis courts at Wigan Park would fill up for two weeks of every year, which was about as close as I'd got to going to Wimbledon in the past. After school I remember getting on my bike and heading over to the courts, although we never did it at any other time in the year.

I'm not even sure I'd had afternoon tea before. Don't get me wrong, I've had Yorkshire tea in the afternoon, but never all the works – scones, sandwiches and the rest – so it was a day of firsts for me at the home of British tennis.

It's an amazing place to watch sport. You're surprisingly close to the players and it's just typically English in every way. I really enjoyed it and I'd definitely go back.

I think Moodos (Lewis Moody) was in the royal box. I didn't make the cut for that – maybe one day! But I was very happy where we were.

Our first real action of the summer, on the pitch, came at

the end of July when Johnno decided to organise a trial match involving players within the squad at the Twickenham Stoop. I'd never played in a game like it before and you could tell by the way I was struggling that I found it hard to come to terms with the concept. All the players were mixed up and I didn't even like being in a different changing room from the other lads and the fact that we wore different kits. I went from being in a tight unit with these lads to playing against them.

It was my first 'game' back since my knee operation and it didn't go that well. I think it contributed to me not being selected for the home game against Wales, but I'll never know for sure. I think it reaffirmed the coaches' belief that my knee needed another week's recovery before I was ready to play. I'd only done two full weeks of training at that stage and the Wales game was less than ten days away.

My back three included David Strettle – who got injured – and Fodes. It wasn't a case of Probables v Possibles as teams have done before – it seemed to be selected randomly. We had a proper warm-up, kicked off and we were even kicking penalties for goal. On the one hand it was deadly serious but on the other I just couldn't get into the match.

Courtney injured his neck not long into the game and was taken off to hospital, so that put a dampener on the whole event for me. Fortunately, he was declared okay later and was able to come to New Zealand for the World Cup. I was thinking, 'Oh my God, we're trying to do a bit of training and this is what's happening.' Injuries tend to occur in training games like this when you play a game and people are half there, half not. It was also my first run-out after my knee operation so I was slightly wary of that. All in all, not a great day.

Brian Smith spoke to me about it afterwards and suggested I might have been lethargic. I couldn't disagree and I think they knew I wasn't that keen on the concept.

The coaches weren't upset with my attitude but seemed to understand that I'd found it difficult to play with normal match intensity against my England team-mates. But I think it's something England may do again, so I need to get my head around it for next time.

No sooner had we left the pitch at the Stoop than a gang of us were on our way to Scotland for Mike Tindall's wedding to Zara Phillips. I certainly went to a few places last summer that I never imagined I would when I was growing up in Wigan! It seems only a few minutes ago that I was turning out for Orrell St James and now there I was at a wedding standing next to the Queen.

People often ask me what Mike and Zara are like. Tins has been in the squad for as long as I've played and you couldn't meet a more down-to-earth couple than those two. I've met both Prince Harry and William a few times and they're both really good lads, so normal it's incredible. It's the same with Tins and Zara. He's a Northern lad like me so that helps, I suppose.

The wedding was an event I'll never forget and to be a few feet away from the Queen was pretty surreal. Tins had selected

Biarritz wing Iain Balshaw as his best man and fellow Gloucester player James Simpson-Daniel (Sinbad) as his groomsman. Tins had been winding Sinbad up all week, telling him Balsh was dropping out and he'd have to step in. But in the end Balsh did really well with his speech. Yes, there was a bit of swearing, but he got all of that out of the way at the start and no one seemed to mind. Cameras were banned and there was no Tweeting from the event. We had a good evening. Obviously Melissa loved the occasion and so did I. Who wouldn't?

We got back into the England camp on the Sunday and I think it was no coincidence that the coaches had a pretty hard session in store for us on the Monday. It was the start of Test week and I think they were saying to us, 'If you overindulged at the wedding, here's a training session to put you back on track.' They didn't need to worry, though, because we all knew it was a serious time – no one was going to use Tins' wedding as an excuse to go mad.

Brian Smith explained to me that I wouldn't play in the first game against Wales, but the plan was for me to play in the second in Cardiff. But I was fully fit for that first match and I took not being selected badly. I couldn't help but see it as being dropped. I understood exactly why I wasn't picked as they wanted to give everyone game time and they also wanted to give my knee an extra week, not that I needed it.

While I understood the reasoning, I couldn't accept it. The three Tests in August would decide if I was going to go to New

Zealand and after finishing the Six Nations without a try in the final three games against France, Scotland and Ireland, I wanted to pull the shirt straight back on and get out there. However, my disappointment at missing the first England v Wales match at Twickenham turned to despair a few days later.

I was picked to play in Cardiff, a week after we beat them 23–19 at Twickenham. But at a training session on the Tuesday before the game I slipped and turned my ankle running to pick a ball up. What a daft injury to pick up. But it shows how quickly your dream of playing for England can disappear.

It was pretty sore immediately. Normally if I roll my ankle – which I've done many times – it is okay but this one just wasn't. I could hardly walk on the Thursday, but I wasn't going to give this one up because it was the final game before Johnno announced the World Cup squad. I tried everything to get fit for this game and even had a very late fitness test, which unfortunately I failed.

It wasn't for lack of trying. I went in the pool for about two days, going swimming about fifteen times, in a bid to get the ankle moving again. It was very painful when we arrived in Cardiff, but I still wasn't prepared to admit I would miss the match. It was driving me mad.

I was feeling under huge pressure to put in performances that would allow me to make the squad. I also wanted games. I'd had my operation at the end of May and it was now August and I hadn't played a proper rugby match. I'd trained and I'd taken part in the trial match but it's almost impossible to replicate match fitness, and I could see time running out before we went to New Zealand.

It was really frustrating for me that I hadn't played. I wanted to get on with it and get back into it again. After missing the first Wales game I was mentally ready to go, but my ankle wouldn't let me. I couldn't train properly and the injury distracted me from the game and stopped me getting mentally right for it.

We did a fitness test on the day of the game. We went down to this little patch of grass where the team were going to walk through some moves and it just wasn't moving right. It was close and I was pleased with how close I managed to get it in such a short space of time. But a few seconds into the fitness test I knew I wouldn't be able to play.

It was a real shame because I felt my normal self again. We'd had an open training session at Twickenham that week and in that session I'd felt strong. The physios tried to reassure me that if I'd played I'd have made it worse and made myself look stupid, and while I know they're right it was still frustrating to hear it. I was annoyed at myself that I had let it happen.

As I failed my fitness test I had to go and watch the game from the stands, a game I should have been playing in. I had to go on the coach, sit in the changing rooms, and I ended up sitting next to Riki Flutey, who was the 23rd man, on the bench. He warmed up and then came and sat next to me.

It was the first time I'd gone to a match on the team coach

when I wasn't playing and it's not an experience I want to repeat. It was a strange environment to be in. I had no role at all. I just sat around, wished a few lads good luck, and tried to keep out of the way. There was little else I could do. It was hard to sit there and not be involved.

The team were hugely frustrated with their performance as they hammered on the Wales line without getting the try they deserved, eventually losing 19–9. We'd won the first match and knew we should have won the second one too. You have to give Wales's defence a lot of credit though. They kept us out and we weren't up for finishing that day.

Once the game was over, everyone knew there was nothing more they could do to ensure that they got a place on that plane to New Zealand and that the call would soon come saying if they were in or not.

Some lads know deep down if they're in the squad, but I could never let myself believe I had made it. I never believe great news like that until I actually get told.

So I felt I was in a strange position before the call came because I hadn't played. Had I already done enough? Would Johnno go with the guys who had played in August? These questions and many more were going through my mind after the defeat to Wales.

What was certain was that some of the lads you had shared the summer with would not be there any more. Some had already been sent home but the battle for the final few places had been intense.

Splashdown

Among the players it's a conversation everyone avoids. There's no banter about the squad as no one would want anyone to think they thought they were in the squad before the call came.

One guy who definitely would have been in the squad was scrum-half Danny Care. He was in great form but had – unbeknown to me – picked up a toe injury in the Wales game. He told Fodes after the game that his toe was hurting. But it seemed like a routine injury, and we didn't think anything of it. I noticed he was running awkwardly towards the end of the game but we all thought it wasn't that bad. However, in the days afterwards it sunk in that this was a serious injury and before we knew it the RFU had announced that Danny needed an operation and was out of the World Cup.

Our protocol is to report injuries to the medical team and I believe Danny woke up the next morning and it was very sore, which is when the alarm bells went off. He went for a scan and soon got the dreaded news.

DC is a good friend so to see that happen to him so close to the tournament, after he had gone through all the training and preparation, was soul-destroying. I called him and he told me he was booked in for an operation straightaway. He was upset. We all knew he had a big shot at being the starting scrum-half as the training camp had gone so well for him and he'd followed that up with good performances in the warm-up games. I was annoyed to see that happen, and also I knew I had lost a good friend if I made the trip to New Zealand.

Starting to Get Serious

When I went back to Pennyhill Park, my washing was waiting for me and next to mine was Danny's. So I took great pleasure in taking a picture and posting it on Twitter. I hope he would have done the same for me. I wasn't taking the mickey out of him, honestly.

On the Monday after the Wales game I missed the big call from Johnno and he left a message on my voicemail congratulating me on my inclusion. He allowed me the option to ring back, but Johnno didn't answer so I left him a message saying thanks for the call and that I would see him next week.

I was delighted of course because I'd never dare to presume I'd make a World Cup squad, or any England team for that matter.

Once Johnno's call was made the system was for it to be followed up by another one from either backs coach Brian Smith or forwards coach John Wells, so obviously it was Smithy who called me.

We had the rest of the week off and met up again on the Monday before the final warm-up against Ireland and the big send-off dinner at Twickenham. That week coincided with my older sister Claire's birthday, so the whole family came down from Wigan to Northampton to visit me. I also had a night out in London with some friends. It was my last chance to see everyone for a long time, or at least that's what I hoped.

Those days gave me a chance to get everything ready for the trip because I knew once we returned to the squad there would be no more time until we got on the plane to New Zealand.

Splashdown

The final warm-up game against Ireland was scheduled for the Saturday and we departed for New Zealand two days later. Twenty-nine of the players made the send-off dinner but James Haskell missed the start because he went for a scan of an injury, and there was some horrendous traffic on the M3.

Some people thought it was a bit odd to play a warm-up game once the squad had been announced, but I was delighted it had been arranged because it gave me the chance to play a match before we headed off to the World Cup. It was a good idea to have a game without the players wondering if they were going to the World Cup. Injuries are always in the back of your mind but it's rugby and you can't worry too much about injuries. I always believe if an injury is going to happen it will, and if it's meant to be, it's meant to be. I had to get on with it like any other game.

One thing it wasn't within the squad was a warm-up match. There was a lot of feeling in the squad about the way we had lost to Ireland in Dublin the previous March in the Six Nations. That defeat hurt and not just because it cost us a Grand Slam. So we couldn't wait to get back to Dublin and play again. We were desperate to beat them and I don't think we were ever likely to lose that game.

The forwards, in particular, were playing with a steely determination. We owed Ireland and it was fortunate we got the chance to go there again. The scenario was quite similar in that they were on a losing run again – they were up against it but this time Ireland never got a foothold in the match.

Starting to Get Serious

Even though we won it was another frustrating game for me, not least because I was sent to the sin-bin for killing the ball. It was my first game back and in a normal season that first match would have been a pre-season trip to the South of France with Northampton, to play nothing more than a training game against a local side.

It was so strange to be standing there singing the national anthem for your country at the beginning of the season. It had never been like that before so I knew it wouldn't go exactly to plan. However, I didn't expect to have such little impact on the game. In every game I want to have a massive effect and I set such high standards for myself that I can only be disappointed looking back on it. When games don't go the way I plan I'm so frustrated.

The fact that I had very few chances didn't help my humour after the match. It's up to me to change things. It's up to me to get involved and have an effect on the game, but I couldn't that day in Dublin.

Despite my frustration we ran out good winners, Manu running through the Ireland defence and Delon collecting a clever chip from Tins to score our second try. It was very different to the match at the end of the Six Nations and it was great to get such a convincing victory before getting on the plane to New Zealand.

Looking back, I suppose ten to twelve weeks off is a long time without playing rugby so maybe I should have expected some rustiness. I was chasing the game but it just wasn't coming. It doesn't click sometimes and even though it frustrates me I have to learn to cope with it, get on with the match, and not expect to score three tries in every game. It's hard after scoring all the time for Northampton. The pressure comes from me, not from the coaches who have never got on my back for not scoring.

We won but we did pick up one significant injury in that Mark Cueto had a back spasm when he tried to make a run down the left wing in the first half, an injury that kept him out of the first two games of the World Cup. Luckily we had Delo (Armitage) in the wings and he's a perfect person to fit anywhere in the back three. He'd had a great summer and he's done a good job on the wing.

The experience of going to Dublin five months earlier was a big help. The Irish sing two anthems and although that sounds like a relatively small thing it does increase the delay between us running out and starting the match. This time I was much better prepared for the delay, so it didn't affect me. People try to tell you what is coming from a trip to somewhere like Dublin but you need to experience it yourself to understand it. Sitting in the changing room for that match in August I knew what was coming and it wasn't going to bother me. I knew how they would play at home, I knew about the crowd, I knew everything I needed to know. That hadn't been the case in March; then I had been going into the unknown.

There wasn't much time to celebrate as we had to get on the

plane that night to make it back for our World Cup farewell the next day. But we boarded the plane from Dublin feeling very satisfied as they had beaten us pretty convincingly in March, a defeat that had been hard to take.

The management had planned a family day on the Sunday. Melissa and my mum had been watching the match at the hotel, so were waiting for me when I got back and we had a squad barbecue with a band playing – a lovely day all round, which ended up with Sos (Matt Stevens) on the guitar and Tins singing. Manu also grabbed the guitar and sang his 'first cap' song, which was pretty impressive from him. A good example of how he was developing within the squad.

The Monday was difficult because I hate saying goodbye. Relatives didn't come to the airport, we left them at the hotel. My mum, my sister Beth and Melissa were there waving me goodbye. I didn't even say goodbye to the dog. At home it's just me, Melissa and the dog so he's a big part of our family. When I'd last seen him I'd said, 'See you in a few weeks, pal.' I said 'see you' to Melissa, Beth and Mum like I'd say it if I was seeing them tomorrow, which made it easier for me to cope with.

There were quite a few parents there and it was great to have Mum there. She comes to every game and has been a big part of my rugby from day one, which is why she also made the trip to New Zealand with Melissa and Beth in the campervan. My mum never feels she can say the sort of things my dad would have said. But I think she knows what he would have said and that helps a little.

Before I knew it we were disappearing into the Surrey countryside heading to Heathrow for a tournament I had been waiting years to play in, the most important tournament of my life – the 2011 Rugby World Cup.

Ireland 9 England 20

Ireland
Pens: O'Gara 3
G Murphy; T Bowe, K Earls, G D'Arcy, A Trimble;
R O'Gara, E Reddan; C Healy, J Flannery, M Ross,
D O'Callaghan, P O'Connell (capt), S Ferris, D Wallace,
J Heaslip
Replacements: F McFadden for Trimble (71), J Sexton for
O'Gara (62), C Murray for Reddan (62), T Court for Healy
(70), R Best for Flannery (50), D Leamy for Wallace (22).
D Ryan for Heaslip (35)

England
Tries: Tuilagi, Armitage **Cons:** Wilkinson 2
Pens: Wilkinson 2
B Foden; C Ashton, M Tuilagi, M Tindall (capt), M Cueto;
J Wilkinson, R Wigglesworth; A Sheridan,
S Thompson, D Cole, L Deacon, C Lawes, T Croft,
H Fourie, J Haskell

Replacements: T Flood for Tindall (75), D Armitage for Cueto (21), M Stevens for Sheridan (55), D Hartley for Thompson (52), S Shaw for Deacon (62), T Palmer for Fourie (21)
Sin-bin: Ashton (41)

Referee: N Owens (Wales)
Attendance: 48,523

12

To a Land Down Under

It was a bleary-eyed arrival in the Land of the Long White Cloud. We touched down in New Zealand at 5.30am and it immediately hit me that I had arrived in more ways than one.

From as early as I can remember my dad had talked to me about playing for England and the ultimate accolade of representing my country at the World Cup. And when I looked around that Auckland Airport arrivals lounge at my twenty-nine other team-mates, it struck me how lucky I was to have made it. I resolved that I was going to do everything in my power to get back on that Air New Zealand jumbo jet with the Webb Ellis Cup tucked under my arm.

It was going to be eight weeks away from home, eight weeks

in unfamiliar – perhaps hostile – surroundings, but every fitness session, every weights session and every hill run with the voice of Nick Johnston in my ear would be worth it if I could get my hands on that gold trophy.

Some people enjoy the flights but for me it's a long time to be in the air. The main message was listen to the doctor or you're going to struggle when you get to New Zealand.

The doctor had planned the whole trip for us so as to minimise jet lag and if you're thinking of making the trip I can reveal the best thing (medically anyway) is to stay awake for the first leg to Los Angeles and then sleep in the second leg, effectively turning your watch to New Zealand time the moment you step on the plane. That meant we needed to keep ourselves awake on the first leg any way we could, which involved lots of food and some films, which for me included another viewing of *Wall Street*, and lying in the beds we were fortunate to be provided with on board.

But I still struggled with the flight. When we went to Australia a year earlier, at breakfast we were given these lights to put on that were supposed to simulate daylight.

It wasn't the first time I had gone to New Zealand. I did it first with the England Under-18s rugby league team to play New Zealand. That was an altogether different affair. I was sick twice on that trip and we all travelled in economy. This time we were in business, with flat beds. I was next to Dyl but there was so much space I could hardly see him.

Splashdown

On the rugby league trip all those years ago we had a competition to see who could stay up the longest and by the end you had lads with blankets over their heads with just their eyes showing playing staring games with each other. That's what you had to do – stare at each other for hours on end. It was absolutely horrible in those little seats.

When we got there it was tough too. I was two years younger than most of the other players and the New Zealanders seemed giants to us. Our opponents were men, driving up to the matches in cars. When they first arrived we genuinely thought they were the dads, turning up to support their kids.

I was playing centre at the time. We lost the first Test but in the same way that so many England teams do, we dug in and turned it round for the second Test. That seems to always happen with English rugby. I came off the bench in the second game.

We stayed on a pretty rough estate in Auckland so the contrast couldn't have been greater when I arrived in the capital city this time around, and the team checked into the impressive Sky City Hotel.

It was pretty early when we landed so I was impressed to see that so many people had turned up to welcome us and give us a traditional Maori welcome. The fans were about five or ten deep at the airport, which was pretty good I thought – especially considering the time. Mind you, when the Samoans arrived it was a little different with people dumping their cars on the way to the airport and parking anywhere they could.

The fans were about forty deep for the Samoans, which showed from the off what huge support they received.

Skype is a real godsend for me and many members of the team as we use the video conferencing system to keep in touch with people back home. The eleven-hour time difference does make it harder, though, as it's tough to keep up with the actual time. As soon as I wake up, back home people are getting ready for bed.

In those first few days in Auckland we were encouraged to take things easy. There is some research that suggests running straight off the plane can damage your anterior cruciate ligament joints, so it was time for some light down time early on.

I did go and have a look at the famous SkyJump, which gives you a chance to base-jump by wire off the tallest man-made structure in New Zealand. But in the end I decided to leave the adrenalin activities for Queenstown.

We had one day out in Auckland where we were given the chance to race America's Cup boats in the harbour. Naturally my boat won. We weren't taking it that seriously until we saw Johnno and forwards coach John Wells in the boat next to us. That was all the inspiration we needed to speed up and get over the line first.

We celebrated with a night out for the whole squad and when we were in the restaurant I got talking to this guy who said he was the artist who'd painted the paintings on the wall. Of course I didn't believe him so eventually, to convince me, he said I could have any painting off the wall. Our scrum coach, Graham Rowntree, was there as well and the guy made the same offer to him.

So we took the paintings off the wall as the owner was coming over. 'What are you doing?' the owner snapped, so we explained and called the artist forward and the owner had to accept we could keep them.

To be fair, the owner played it well and hoodwinked us. He said: 'Let's just leave them over there and come back and collect them tomorrow.' Of course he knew we'd never remember and we didn't come back the next day as we were off to Dunedin, the city where we were playing the first game of our World Cup against Argentina . . . minus our paintings.

When we arrived on the South Island I thought Dunedin was a throwback to the 1980s. Carpet on the walls in the lift, for example. But by the time we left I was missing the place and regarding it a bit more like home. The people were so friendly and it helped that we were playing Argentina, rather than New Zealand.

We were told the team on the Monday of the Test week and I was mightily relieved and delighted to be named on the wing. Disappointingly, our captain Lewis Moody hadn't made it as his knee wasn't quite right. Similarly the back spasm Mark Cueto got in the Ireland match hadn't cleared up and he was left on the sidelines too.

In Dunedin, which was our base for much of the first few weeks, we attended the capping ceremony and enjoyed a traditional nose-rubbing Maori welcome, called the hongi. Luckily my cap fitted snugly but Cueto had no chance of getting his on!

However, it was during this week that what we thought was an innocent prank ended up on the front page of a newspaper. It all revolved around us taking walkie-talkies from people at the hotel. Juvenile? You're right, but we never intended it to be malicious. It was something that a few of us had done as they allowed you to speak to the whole staff and anyone else who was listening. Harmless stuff, we thought.

So when one of the hotel workers came to Dyl's bedroom to retrieve her walkie-talkie, the incident occurred, which we believed was some banter between us and a woman we had got to know during our stay.

There is no way we intended to humiliate anyone, which is why we thought we had put the matter to rest. But when we returned to the hotel – after our trip to Queenstown – we were told by Johnno that she was upset. We had no idea there was an issue, so we were all shocked when Johnno called us in to tell us the woman had complained.

We had said things to her such as she couldn't have her walkie-talkie back unless she gave us chocolate. It was on that level and if the remarks were found to be lewd we're very sorry if we offended her.

We offered her a heartfelt apology and a bunch of flowers, but it didn't seem to do any good. Her story later appeared in a newspaper and was then in almost every other media for about forty-eight hours. It even led Johnno to front a massive press conference.

Things are rarely what they seem and that was the case with this story, which we felt was blown out of all proportion.

Our attention was soon back focused on rugby and we went to see our team room in the new Otago Stadium before our first game. And it was an incredible sight, the first indoor rugby stadium in the world. The Millennium Stadium has a roof of course but this stadium is permanently enclosed, with a glass roof like a greenhouse, which is how the locals refer to it. The noise from the fans in there was immense and although the pitch was a little narrower than we're used to, we knew it would be a great place to play, and we had three games there.

The whole occasion was great and I certainly hadn't seen so many Argentinian fans in one place as I did that night. Their passion and the noise they make is magnificent. It was a little like the Millennium Stadium in that it was very hard to hear what your team-mates had to say.

Crucially we made a winning start, though we had to really work for it. I knew World Cup matches would be tight but I never thought we would lose the game, even though we trailed 9–3 with fifteen minutes remaining. England have had some great battles with the Pumas over the years and with their subsequent win over Scotland, which took them into the quarter-finals, Argentina showed what a good team they are.

They finished third in 2007 so they had our respect coming into this tournament and proved as difficult to beat as we imagined.

Even though we won, it was another frustrating day for me as I didn't get any chances to score. The game was my fifth successive one without a try and although the dry run wasn't bothering my team-mates or management, and we were winning, it was definitely bothering me.

Over the year or so I had played for England, Martin Johnson had rarely had cause to sit down and have a chat with me, despite people suggesting he'd hauled me over the coals for diving. But he could see the barren run was getting to me so we sat down to talk it over.

He told me how the same thing had happened to Iain Balshaw when he broke into the England team. He scored a hatful of tries early on and then had to be patient, before finally being part of the squad that won the World Cup in 2003. These runs do happen, I know that, but I also know I need to relax in the run-up to games and during the matches. I know I mustn't force things or try too hard. I can get distracted by trying too hard to score tries and I need to work that out of my game.

It was good of Johnno to spare the time for that one-on-one and it was reassuring to know there was no pressure on me from above to score. The team had won and ultimately that is all that matters.

Splashdown

England 13 Argentina 9

England
Try: Youngs **Con:** Wilkinson **Pens:** Wilkinson 2
B Foden; C Ashton, M Tuilagi, M Tindall (capt), D Armitage;
J Wilkinson, R Wigglesworth; A Sheridan, S Thompson,
D Cole, L Deacon, C Lawes, T Croft, J Haskell, N Easter
Replacements: B Youngs for Wigglesworth (50), M Stevens
for Sheridan (62), D Hartley for Thompson (62), T Palmer
for Deacon (65)
Sin-bin: Cole (34)

Argentina
Pens: Contepomi, Rodriguez 2
Rodriguez; G Camacho, G Tiesi, Fernandez, Agulla;
F Contepomi (capt), Vergallo; Roncero, M Ledesma, Figallo,
Carizza, Albacete, Farias Cabello, Leguizamon, Fernandez
Lobbe
Replacements: Imhoff for Tiesi (36), Bosch for Contepomi
(26), Creevy for Ledesma (56), M Scelzo for Figallo (57),
Campos for Cabello (69), Galarza for Leguizamon (79)

Attendance: 30,700
Referee: Bryce Lawrence (New Zealand)

The day after we beat Argentina we travelled to Queenstown
for a couple of days off and some training in the run-up to the

238

Georgia match. We were all allowed a night out on the Sunday and unfortunately ours ended in us being splashed across the front page of the *Sun* newspaper later in the week.

There was nothing wrong in what we did. All that happened was that we had a drink and a joke with some people who were in the bar. There was nothing in it, we were simply having a night out like anyone else would and letting off a bit of steam.

The publicity was incredible really as all we did was go out for a few drinks. There was even the ludicrous suggestion we took part in some bizarre dwarf-throwing competition. That never happened, although there were some little people in the pub – the only thing a few of the boys did was have their photos taken with them. Mike Tindall got most of the flak but that's because he's married to Zara Phillips. Sadly, the attention he got is a reality of his life now.

We had a chat about it as a squad, naturally, and it pulled us closer together, but it wasn't a big deal in Johnno's mind: I loved one quote he gave to the media: 'Rugby players drink beer – shocker!'

Eight weeks in New Zealand is pretty intense and it came after the best part of three months in camp, so we're entitled to have a couple of nights out.

I've always seen the value of rugby teams going out for a few beers together. It's a good way of relaxing, getting to know people better. When you play for England there's a lot of attention on you for large parts of your day, so socialising with the lads is a good way of releasing some of the tension that can build up at a tournament like the World Cup.

The day after our night out was a day off for the boys and I was determined to enjoy the down time, especially after what had been an intense start to our World Cup campaign. I hooked up with Dyl, Fodes, Nick Easter, James Haskell, Simon Shaw, Richard Wigglesworth and Lewis Moody to take on the Awesome Foursome in Queenstown, which involves a helicopter ride, the Nevis Bungy Swing, the Shotover Jet and Rafting.

I'd never done a bungy jump before, let alone one like the Nevis Bungy, which is New Zealand's highest and 134 metres high. It's fair to say most of the boys jumped with gusto but our skipper Lewis wasn't, shall we say, exactly comfortable with heights, and after going green succumbed to peer pressure to finally leap off . . . luckily he survived.

It was the same for Minty (Nick Easter) and Wiggy (Richard Wigglesworth). I don't think any of the three of them will be doing it again, although afterwards Lewis and Wiggy said they were glad we bullied them into doing it. Wiggy at least had a plan and told the guy running it that the only way he was going to do it was if he pushed him off, which he duly did.

It wasn't quite as problematic for me. I did the Nevis four times, and I think I now have an addiction to adrenalin sports, although sky diving was off limits because it's regarded as too dangerous by the England management, along with skiing.

Well, when you get the chance I believe in living life to the full. James Haskell matched me by doing it four times as well.

Johnno was more than happy for us to enjoy ourselves on our day off. There were still six days to go before we played Georgia and if all we did at the World Cup was train, play and train I think there would have been a big danger of us getting stale. Rest and recuperation are crucial factors in any World Cup campaign.

We did the white-water rafting first, which was good fun but the water was freezing. As soon as the guide told us we could get off we all jumped in but it was so cold, basically melted ice. Minty seemed to take on the role of ship's captain on the raft, sitting in the middle and doing nothing while we worked hard to keep away from the rocks.

I know we got criticised for doing some of those activities, mainly from people back home, but once we had made the decision to have a day off we needed to do it properly.

Training in Queenstown was terrific as we were in the shadow of the Remarkables mountain range, an incredible backdrop for us. We were out of single rooms and into apartments and I was sharing with Ben Youngs and Joe Simpson. We decided to flip a coin for the biggest bedroom, although as it was Joe's first tour with England, Youngsy and I said he didn't qualify so it just came down to me and the Leicester scrum-half . . . and I lost. I knew I should have made it more complicated than the toss of a coin!

It made it worse that Youngsy plays for Leicester so that

meant a Tiger got the better of me. I was left to grumble on my own in my small room with a tiny TV while Youngsy swanned around in his giant room with en suite bathroom and incredible views of the lake.

The only massive downside of Queenstown was the confirmation in the middle of the week that we had lost our first player to injury – Andrew Sheridan.

Sheri had worked so hard to get back from a number of big injuries and I was hoping he'd have as good a World Cup as he did in 2007, when he was a key reason for England beating Australia in the quarter-finals. But in our first game he damaged his shoulder again and was in for a scan and on the way home before we knew it. I admired the way he trained and worked so hard to get fit for the World Cup and it looked to me that he had timed it just right, but clearly fate wasn't on his side.

There was more fallout to come from our win over Argentina because Courtney Lawes was cited for an incident in the first half when he tackled Pumas hooker Mario Ledesma. I looked at the video and couldn't see an awful lot in it, but unfortunately the disciplinary officer didn't agree with me and promptly banned the big lad for two games, putting him out of the matches against Georgia and Romania.

Courtney's ban was a big negative for us but the mood in the camp was good. Argentina were the seeded team in our pool and we'd started off by beating them. One job done, more to come!

13

Making the Quarter-Finals

We had passed our first test of the World Cup by beating Argentina, and none of us had been taking that one for granted. But with the Pumas behind us it was time to refocus our efforts on the remaining pool matches against Georgia, Romania and, the big one, Scotland. We knew these three games could not only define this World Cup but could define our careers as rugby players.

The win was the important thing against Argentina but I left the ground frustrated as I drew another blank in terms of scoring tries, which meant I spent most of the start of the Georgia week annoyed.

I had to keep reminding myself that, following my knee and ankle injuries, the Argentina game was only my second of the season, but it's not how I wanted my World Cup career to start. It does take a few weeks to get back into it, even though you deny it. It takes a few games to get used to running around and being in position again.

I know we won, I know the Pumas are a good side and difficult to play against – Johnno has said that a number of times and I know he's right. But I was still frustrated with my own game. It wasn't where I wanted it to be.

It wasn't just not scoring that annoyed me. It was a messy match and I spent most of my time chasing around trying to get involved, without getting very far. I hate it when games are like that and I wasn't in a good mood afterwards. To be honest, I was pretty cranky. Fodes (Ben Foden) was saying: 'Come on, mate, we won,' and I just sat there saying, 'Yeah, whatever.'

The England boys would all like to be able to play a bit more but teams are going to try to stop us. I watched the Australia game and Italy did it to them for about fifty minutes, then it opened up. Argentina were winning for a long, long time, but I never thought we'd lose.

Johnno told us before we left England that he wanted us to get out into the New Zealand community on this trip, to meet the locals, and this week that entailed a visit to meet the kids from Arrowtown Primary School, who became England fans for the day. I really love getting kids involved in rugby.

Dyl, Mark Cueto, Alex Corbisiero, James Haskell and

myself landed at the school by helicopter, which I thought was a little over the top and a little too Bond-like for me, but the kids seemed to like it, which is the main thing.

They greeted us with a haka powhiri and after a rendition of the traditional welcoming song, 'Tihei Mauri Ora', we were greeted by the school's sports teacher, Paul Winders.

After the haka – which Cuets accepted on our behalf – the kids set us a challenge which I've never been faced with before: a Shredded Wheat eating contest. We were set the task of eating one large Shredded Wheat in the quickest time. It doesn't sound difficult but doing it without any liquid to accompany it makes it a different proposition altogether.

They told us – although I didn't believe it – that Richie McCaw scoffed one in fifteen seconds, but it's fair to say we struggled. Clark Kent – or Alex Corbisiero as he's better known – was the best out of us and even he took forty-seven seconds. It took me well over a minute.

That was a great respite from training and the preparation for the Georgia game, which we knew would be tough, despite what people back home thought.

Looking through the Georgia team you'll see players from many French clubs and they even had Mamuka Gorgodze, who was voted the best foreign player in the Top 14 last season. That's right, the league that has Jonny Wilkinson and Carl Hayman in it.

They're one of the up-and-coming teams in world rugby and were reigning champions of what is effectively the second division of the Six Nations, so we knew they would be a tough nut to crack. They were all big lads and they ran at you head first and tackled as if their lives depended on it.

The game was on a Sunday so we flew back to Dunedin on the Friday in a tiny chartered plane. In New Zealand there's no train network like there is in England so everyone takes planes like they would trains. Most of these planes are tiny and although I didn't mind doing the Nevis Bungy, I wasn't too happy about flying what I considered low in this plane. It was very bumpy and I felt sick the whole way. The flight was only about twenty-five minutes long but it was up and down, up and down.

We arrived to have our team run, and the game on Sunday.

We ended up winning the game 41–10 but it was a real struggle and I was chuffed to score two tries. I hadn't scored for five games and it was starting to prey on my mind so I was delighted to get my first World Cup try, so delighted I couldn't help but celebrate with a dive, especially as I ran in from forty metres out.

I'm not sure people were too impressed and it may not have been the right time considering how the game unfolded, but I thought it was time to celebrate. As I ran in I saw it as the perfect opportunity.

To score a try in a World Cup is a massive achievement for me. It was a sensational feeling to get that first one and I wanted to make sure I played well too. I hadn't done myself justice in the Argentina game but against Georgia I felt back to my usual self. I'm not saying that because I scored – I was just pleased with my overall performance.

My second try wasn't as successful. I scored right on the final whistle, at the corner, and as I touched down one of the Georgia players dived on me. He came down with such force that if I hadn't got my arm out of the way I think he would have dislocated or broken the elbow. So I suppose I was lucky, even if it was still sore two weeks later. It was a heavy blow.

We knew we had to deal with Georgia's size in the contact area by moving them around, but we failed to do that, although I thought the match did a job of restoring some of our confidence.

It was another win, but no one in the squad was particularly happy with the performance and we heard that in the post-match press conference Johnno had admitted he was angry. We gave away far too many penalties (fourteen) against Georgia and the reality is that if their kicker, Merab Kvirikashvili, had been on song, we'd have been behind at half-time. So I think the coaches felt enough was enough.

Johnno said that considering what had already happened on the tour, now was the time to have a quiet night in, and we all agreed to stay in the hotel bar for the whole evening.

On the Monday after the game, we had a team meeting. I believe it was long overdue, because many of us felt we were leaving a lot of points out on the field.

Splashdown

Mike Ford, our defence coach, led the talking and he spoke passionately about the way we were letting everyone down with the penalty count. As most of them came when we were defending he felt it was his fault.

He gave what I like to call his *Gladiator* speech, something I'd never seen from Fordy before. He told us if we were going to do well at this World Cup, it was time to draw a line in the sand.

I think that was the moment when everyone in the room realised we weren't going to get any more chances at the World Cup, and that our tournament could be over very quickly unless we improved.

Jonny Wilkinson spoke after him and spoke well, saying he was disappointed that Mike had even needed to raise the subject as we should all know better – there was complete agreement. We all do know that deep down but sometimes you forget and need reminding.

The good thing is that there is complete honesty in the England squad about things like this, so names were named and people shown to have made mistakes asked to explain why they made them. If you're going to move forward, it's crucial you have a level of honesty in a squad.

It was an excellent meeting and from then on we decided we had used up all our chances and our resolve was tightened.

We talked about how we needed to remove all distraction for these final weeks of this World Cup and leave no stone unturned in our pursuit of the ultimate goal. That was driven by captain Lewis Moody and one of the senior players, Mike Tindall.

England 41 Georgia 10

England
Tries: Hape 2, Ashton 2, Armitage, Tuilagi **Cons:** Flood 4
Pen: Flood
B Foden; C Ashton, M Tuilagi, S Hape, D Armitage;
T Flood, B Youngs; M Stevens, D Hartley, D Cole, S Shaw,
T Palmer, T Wood, L Moody, J Haskell
Replacements: M Banahan for Tuilagi (67), J Simpson for
Youngs (67), D Cole for Stevens (74), S Thompson for
Hartley (60), A Corbisiero for Cole (63), S Thompson for
Wood (temp 39–48), T Croft for Moody (57)
Sin-bin: Hartley (39)

Georgia
Try: Basilaia **Con:** Kvirikashvili **Pen:** Kvirikashvili
R Gigauri; I Machkhaneli, D Kacharava, T Zibzibadze,
S Todua; M Kvirikashvili, I Abuseridze (capt);
D Khinchagashvili, J Bregvadze, D Kubriashvili, I Zedginidze,
V Maisuradze, S Sutiashvili, M Gorgodze, D Basilaia
Replacements: L Khmaladze for Machkhaneli (40),
L Datunashvili for Todua (67), B Samkharadze for
Abuseridze (63), G Shvelidze for Khinchagashvili (56),
D Zirakashvili for Kubriashvili (27), L Datunashvili for

Splashdown

Zedginidze (temp 6–16), G Chkhaidze for Sutiashvili (31),
G Berishvili for Basilaia (60)

Referee: J Kaplan (South Africa)
Attendance: 20,117

A hat-trick is always very pleasing but me scoring any tries at
all seemed a long way away at the start of our third pool game
against Romania. While I wasn't seeing much of the ball, Mark
Cueto ran in three tries in eleven minutes. It was good to have
the old man back in the team and I'm delighted for him that
he scored some tries after his injury.

Cuets had been so unlucky to pick up that freak back injury
against Ireland in August. You can train as much as you want
but, as I know only too well, you're never fully with it until
you've got a game under your belt, so I'm glad it went the way
it did for him.

I have a great rapport with Cuets and I think it's natural to
have that with someone you've played with so many times – he
has been there for almost every game of my England career.

Sometimes it happens with players, sometimes it doesn't.
You just tend to click, as Cuets and I have done. I can't tell you
why that is, it's just how it's been since we've played together –
perhaps it's because we're two Northern boys together? We
kind of know what's going to happen, when each of us gets the
ball. With Cuets, I can swap wings and comfortably sit on
either side of the pitch.

That rapport meant I was able to stay relatively relaxed when he had three tries and I had none. But I wanted a try at some point and thankfully the lads put me in for a few.

Set plays only tend to come off if Manu's steamrolling it straight up the middle, not for an inside ball for me. I try to get on Manu's inside when he storms through. Most players look for an offload, but every time Manu goes through he just scores! It's useless for me!

Seriously, this game showed what a massive impact Manu has had on the whole team. Sometimes you just need a person you can rely on, someone who's going to hit the ball hard and get you moving forward again. We've got Tins there as well but Manu's just got that extra spice about him. Especially when you're new to playing international rugby, you've just got that added oomph, you want to give it everything. He definitely gave it everything at this World Cup. Every time he gets the ball he looks a danger.

I'd rather Manu makes the breaks and I'm just there inside. It's his job to go flying into people – and he's pretty good at it as well. He put Fodes in against Romania so he's getting the hang of setting them up as well as scoring them.

We went into the Romania game in good spirits as we had continued not only taking – as the cliché says – one game at a time, but we were exactly where we wanted to be.

Splashdown

England 67 Romania 3

England
Tries: Cueto 3, Ashton 3, Youngs, Foden, Tuilagi, Croft
Cons: Wilkinson 3, Flood 4 **Pen:** Wilkinson
B Foden; C Ashton, M Tuilagi, M Tindall, M Cueto;
J Wilkinson, B Youngs; A Corbisiero, S Thompson, D Cole,
L Deacon, T Palmer, T Croft, L Moody (capt), J Haskell
Replacements: D Armitage for Foden (52), T Flood for
Wilkinson (h-t), R Wigglesworth for Youngs (60), D Cole
for Corbisiero (58), L Mears for Thompson (50), D Wilson
for Cole (h-t), S Shaw for Deacon (58), T Wood for Moody
(66)

Romania
Pen: Dumbrava
F Vlaicu; S Ciuntu, I Cazan, I Dumitras, A Apostol;
D Dumbrava, L Sirbu; N Nere, B Zebega, S Florea,
V Poparlan, C Petre (capt), S Burcea, C Ratiu, O Tonita
Replacements: C Nicolae for Vlaicu (71), C Gal for Cazan
(42), V Calafeteanu for Sirbu (h-t), M Tincu for Zebega
(50), P Ion for Florea (61), M Macovei for Petre (52),
D Ianus for Ratiu (59)

Referee: R Poite (France)
Attendance: 25,687

Straight after the Romania game we headed off to watch New Zealand take on France. The All Blacks were so clinical in their finishing and offload ability – it was very impressive.

It was clear from this game that if you want to stop New Zealand you've got to stop them offloading. Those key players, like Ma'a Nonu, create so much for them. But that's something you've got to look at when you come up against them. The French just weren't with it for so much of the game.

In our World Cup warm-up camp in the summer, Johnno had talked about any of us 'getting a taxi home' if we didn't want to do the hard work and as we started preparing for Scotland it was a similar theme. He was ramming home to us the fact that if we got it wrong against Scotland we'd be picking up our boarding passes on Sunday and heading for a game against 'Newcastle' on the following Friday.

Incredibly, the Scotland game was our first outdoors in the tournament. The first three had been held in the new indoor stadium in Dunedin and now it was off to Eden Park. Moving outdoors was more talked about outside the squad as we just took it in our stride. We're playing rugby, not cricket, so you have to play when it rains and it's windy; and don't forget we had been training outside.

The game against Scotland also saw us decamp to New Zealand's biggest city, Auckland. I enjoyed my time in Dunedin, but it was good to go back to Auckland, if just for a change of scenery. It was good to go to the heart of the action, where the World Cup was most 'happening', and immediately it was clear the atmosphere in Auckland was a lot different to Dunedin, which ultimately is a small town.

I know many people were saying the match against Scotland was the 'real' start of the tournament, but that was a bit harsh, particularly on Georgia and Argentina, who really tested us.

I know what they meant, though, in that this was the first time in the tournament when we could have been knocked out. But my view was the tournament had started three weeks earlier against Argentina – for us especially because it was such a hard game.

Our days off were becoming few and far between, but in Auckland we were lucky enough to be taken out for a driving day by Land Rover, who are a World Cup sponsor.

But I made a huge error and I'm not sure how it happened. In the confusion of leaving our hotel in central Auckland I let Lee Mears get in the driver's seat.

Now I get bored driving, let alone sitting in the passenger seat! Bored to the extent that I cannot, repeat cannot, be trusted with navigating, even when we had a Sat Nav in the car. How can that happen? I think we went wrong at the first set of lights out of the hotel and it got worse from there. Only someone who is cruel would suggest that it was Mearsy's fault because he couldn't see over the steering wheel! I'd never say that, of course. Inevitably I got the blame, but Mearsy was driving so how does that work?

We eventually found the others at Muriwai Beach, near Auckland, but only after I pushed the Bath hooker out of the driving seat and took over. We got there in half an hour, but all the other cars were already a long way up the beach. After five minutes we could see them – they were all in a row and I just went straight past, flying along.

We went on a helicopter flight with a pilot who worked on *Lord of the Rings*. He took us really low, just above the cars, and he was doing some outrageous stuff. Then we went off-roading through the forest.

It was after the Scotland game that I learned I was going to be one of three players, with James Haskell and Dylan Hartley, who were going to be the subject of a front-page story in the *Sunday Mirror* newspaper.

I had never been on the front page before. As rugby players we want to be starring on the back pages, scoring tries, so it's never good to discover you will be on the front pages under the headline: 'England rugby players in more hot water after hotel worker claims she was victim of crude sexual banter.' It went on to say that myself, Dyl and James Haskell had humiliated a woman at our hotel in Dunedin.

I was able to tell my mum and Melissa, who had arrived in New Zealand, in person about the newspaper story. We spoke for half an hour and it was hard telling them I was going to be in the headlines but I was glad I had the chance to talk to my family face to face about it.

It made me very wary for the rest of the trip, made me think twice about talking to people during the World Cup, and certainly made me think twice about having any banter with people I didn't know. I thought it wasn't advisable to go out on my own but if we went out in groups that also brought attention, so there was no way of winning.

Our preparations were good going into the match, although I suppose you don't know whether off-field issues like this have taken a mental toll.

We also had to face Scotland without two of our coaches, Dave Alred and Paul Stridgeon, our fitness coach who everyone calls Bobby, after Bobby Boucher in *The Waterboy*, as that is the job he does for England on match days – he carries the water on.

Dave works mainly with the kickers so I don't really see his influence directly, but Bobby is a key member of the backroom staff, not just for his knowledge as a fitness guy but because he's so positive. He brings a great energy to the side on and off the pitch, and every side needs people like him. It was strange not to have him around when we took on Scotland.

There are many unseen characters in the England set-up and Bobby is one of those and he was really missed on the day of the Scotland game. Other people can take the warm-up instead of him, but it's very difficult to replace the enthusiasm and energy that he brings to the team. If people are down or nervous, Bobby is the first one to pick them up.

The two of them were banned by the RFU after an investigation into the balls that we used to kick in the Georgia game. I had no idea until this happened that there are eight numbered rugby balls used for every World Cup match and the laws of the game state that you must kick the conversion with the ball with which you have scored the try. Twice they unsuccessfully tried to swap it for another ball before Jonny took his conversion. I have no idea why you aren't allowed to do that, if you're unhappy with a particular ball. But the referee spotted it in the Georgia game and before we knew it an investigation had begun and the two coaches were banned for one game.

My view is that a ball is a ball so let the kicker use any one he wants to. But they were deemed to be 'in contravention of both the laws of the game and the spirit of the game' after an internal review, which as players we have to accept.

On the pitch we finished our pool stage in the best place possible – in top position. We confirmed our place after beating Scotland 16–12, staying unbeaten in the pool with only one try conceded – the best defensive record in the tournament. So I'm not sure what all the fuss was about back home. I know we created one or two headlines we would rather not have appeared, but the focus before and after the Scotland game was on the rugby. It has to be. We went to New Zealand to do a job and nothing could have diverted us from that.

We only went into the lead two minutes from time when I got over in the corner, following a superb cut-out pass from Toby Flood. The game followed a similar pattern to the one against Argentina. We never assume that a game is going to go just how we want to play. You must adapt to the conditions.

After the way Scotland frustrated us in the Six Nations, it

continued in the World Cup. It was very windy at Eden Park, so it was hard work, especially under the high ball. Fair play to Scotland, they did what they wanted to do, messing up the play. The scrums, the breakdowns – everything was a mess.

Sometimes you've just got to be patient. We didn't play the way we wanted to play and the game didn't go how we wanted. But sometimes you've got to get yourself out of a hole. Youngsy did it against Argentina and thankfully I was on the end of the decisive move this time.

To illustrate how frustrating the game was, it was fifty-nine minutes and forty seconds before I touched the ball. That's incredible when you think about it, and shows how tight this game was. I can't remember the last time I went that long in a game without touching the ball. At the time I was thinking, 'This is one of the strangest games ever for me, but I've got to get used to it because these games are only going to get worse.'

I can't understand how it happened that way. I was running around hitting a lot of breakdowns, which I'm not very good at, although it's a case of anything for the team. I was trying to get the ball, but the first touch was a kick to the corner, the second touch was another kick and the third touch was my try.

I get frustrated when I'm not involved but it's the World Cup, it was a very tense game with a huge amount at stake, and Scotland had to do what they had to do. That's how it's going to be. Thankfully I got on the end of that one near the finish.

Making the Quarter-Finals

We also saw Jonny miss one or two kicks, which is unusual, but don't forget when he had to he nailed a crucial drop-goal (off his weaker foot) to make it 6–12 and really take the pressure off us. Scotland had to beat us by eight points to progress at our expense.

Jonny is Jonny; in his head he's going to get every kick. No matter where it is he's going to go for it. If Moodos and Tins agree then they're going to keep letting him kick, but as Moodos said after the game perhaps he should have taken the pressure off him and asked him to put some in the corner where we could have taken a lineout.

There is a fine line between going for the corner or going for the posts. I think Jonny was unfortunate on the first few kicks, there were one or two drop-goals thrown in as well.

The game was just so scrappy that you lose a bit of confidence with it, and you feel it's such a close game that you need to take those opportunities. Maybe if we had moved the ball around a bit more we could have got more confidence and go-forward.

My try against Scotland took me to the top of the tournament try-scoring charts with six, but that really was the least of my priorities. That was something for looking back on, not while the tournament was going on.

Now it was time to forget about how many tries I had scored in the pool stage because none of that mattered when we entered the knockout stage against France.

Splashdown

England 16 Scotland 12

England
Try: Ashton **Con:** Flood **Pens:** Wilkinson 2
Drop-goal: Wilkinson
B Foden; C Ashton, M Tuilagi, M Tindall, D Armitage;
J Wilkinson, B Youngs; M Stevens, S Thompson, D Cole,
L Deacon, C Lawes, T Croft, L Moody (capt) J Haskell
Replacements: T Flood for Tindall (71), M Banahan for
Wilkinson (75), R Wigglesworth for Youngs (73),
A Corbisiero for Stevens (72), D Hartley for Thompson
(67), T Palmer for Lawes (56), N Easter for Moody
(temp 53–62), N Easter for Haskell (62)

Scotland
Pens: Paterson 2, Parks **Drop-goal:** Parks
C Paterson; M Evans, J Ansbro, S Lamont, S Danielli;
R Jackson, M Blair; A Jacobsen, R Ford, E Murray, R Gray,
A Kellock (capt), A Strokosch, J Barclay, R Vernon
Replacements: N De Luca for Evans (h-t), D Parks for
Jackson (5), C Cusiter for Blair (71), A Dickinson for
Jacobsen (67), N Hines for Strokosch (64), R Rennie for
Barclay (64)

Referee: C Joubert (South Africa)
Attendance: 58,213

14

The World Cup Exit

Going out of the World Cup at the quarter-final stage was the most gut-wrenching feeling of my career. I was devastated by our exit, it's as simple as that – my worst day in rugby, whether in union or league.

Sitting in the changing rooms at Eden Park at the end of the match I was silent; I couldn't speak. All around me there was desolation. Players in various states of undress, kit, bandages and strappings were all over the floor.

No one spoke and I wondered whether anyone would. Normally when you lose, someone will break the ice with some banter, but no one had the heart to say anything.

For me, sitting in my cubicle, I was frozen to the spot. The dressing-room scene was going on all around me but for me time was standing still. I was aware of some noise, but I had no idea what it was. It was as if I was sitting there and the world was going past in slow motion.

I was aware of Martin Johnson standing in the dressing room speaking, but I had no idea what he was saying, and no recall of it later. He may as well have been speaking French. I had a ringing sound in my ears.

Time ticked by and I started to realise what had happened. We had lost a rugby match we all believed we would win and within forty-eight hours we would be on a plane back to England.

I thought about my dad, as I always do, and perhaps that brought me to my senses because now our captain Lewis Moody was standing in front of us, addressing all the players.

How Moodos found the strength to pick himself up and speak to us I have no idea. But it's the mark of the man that he was able to. I have no doubt that, as captain, he was feeling worse than any of us and he confirmed that when I spoke to him later. But a guy I'd been next to on the pitch was now speaking to us.

I heard him. He spoke very well, as I'm sure Johnno did. Moodos told us to remember the pain we were feeling now, not to ignore it but to take it with us back to England and use it as a weapon to drive us on until we were fortunate enough to pull on the white shirt again.

Eventually I went and sat in the Jacuzzi that was in the changing room. I was numb. It was all I could think of doing, before getting changed as quickly as I could. It was hard to accept.

The World Cup Exit

Through our disappointment I was appreciative of the support we had from England fans, those who travelled to New Zealand and who watched it, in their millions, back home. The crowd makes the atmosphere at a game and where would we be without them? We didn't go as far as we wanted to in New Zealand but I hope the fans understand how all of us were so grateful for their support. It was expensive to make the journey to New Zealand and I felt humbled by their commitment.

The quarter-final was my eighteenth cap but the first time I had lost in knockout rugby. In the Six Nations there is always the chance to come back a week later and even when we lost the final championship match in 2011 we still won the trophy. But this, well, this was different. It was the end and there was nothing I could do about it.

We had come to Eden Park a few hours earlier with a spring in our step and a belief that it was us – and not France – who would be returning to Eden Park a week later to play Wales in the semi-finals.

How it didn't happen still baffles me and always will, even if I'm lucky enough to play for England again in a World Cup. I'm not sure I'll ever forget the feeling I had in that dressing room, and not because of what Moodos had said. It's ingrained in my mind and will stay there and drive me on.

Something else that annoyed me was the fact that everyone had written us off and given us a hard time, and now they would be able to say they were right.

We had been referred to as a stag-do and what certain people have written, others will believe. But nothing could be further from the truth. Considering the amount of effort we put into this World Cup it was hard to take.

In the run-up to the game the England management had to make a big call over Mike Tindall. He's a great leader and organiser for us and is always a big influence on me and the rest of the team, but he had picked up a dead leg in the win over Scotland. This meant Tins couldn't train in the early part of the week and it was decided to pair Jonny Wilkinson and Toby Flood together at outside-half and inside-centre.

I feel safe with Tins there and he's a guiding hand for me, especially on defence. No disrespect to the others, but I missed having him there.

I knew Tins hadn't been selected before the team was announced because I could see the way he was – I sensed he had been told on the Tuesday, even though the team wasn't announced to us until twenty-four hours later. Tins wasn't himself and was really down so it looked to me like he had taken the decision pretty badly, just as I would have done in his position. I could see he was pretty rattled, so although I didn't talk to him about it, I tried to get him up in other ways by having a joke with him. It's not really a conversation I like having with my team-mates. I'd rather focus on something else, because I've been in that position before, although not in a game as important as a World Cup quarter-final.

The World Cup Exit

Johnno doesn't tend to explain the rationale behind a change – the team goes up, that is it and we get on with it.

Don't get me wrong, we thought it would work and no one in that team room had any doubt we would beat France. But as we know now, that didn't happen. Perhaps the team hadn't been playing as well as we could have but we had still been winning.

I wasn't worried because I know the type of player Floody is. He's the type of player who can add to any team and I wasn't disappointed when those names went up. I knew each of those twenty-one guys in the squad alongside me so well that I had complete faith in them to get the job done – no question about that.

Johnno did the same as he always does, telling our video analyst Mike Hughes: 'Stick the team up, Mike.'

We didn't train as intensely as we had done earlier in the tournament, but that is normal. As you come to the knockout stages you expect to taper your training down a little.

Looking back it's hard to work out if we made any mistakes. At the time it seemed absolutely fine and the week was going well, but when you lose a game as big as the one against France you have to analyse it, you have to question whether you did the right thing.

We had trained so hard and there comes a point when there are only a few weeks to go. We could only plan presuming we'd make the final, and also we were training on the back of a very physical game against Scotland. The lads were sore and you have to give them time to rest, but it's a hard thing to manage. We were given Monday off as opposed to a later day in the week, to help our recovery.

It was the biggest week of my rugby life and looking back I was pleased with the way I approached and dealt with it as I tried to deal with it like any other.

I had learned from the Ireland game in the Six Nations and the way I had got more and more tense as the week had gone on. I like to think I now have a bit more experience and I know what's affecting me and what isn't, so I felt really relaxed and didn't focus too much on the game itself.

I try to make sure I enjoy the week of a Test because that's when I play better. I think some people lose sight of that. It's the reason why we're here – we play rugby because we enjoy it.

In the run-up to our quarter-final against France, another incident put us in the headlines for the wrong reason when Manu Tuilagi was fined for wearing a branded gumshield in a match, which is against World Cup rules. Later on Moodos and Courtney were also fined. All gumshields need to be plain. Manu's brother Alesana, a wing for Samoa, had already suffered the same fate, but how on earth was Manu to know there was a rule about having a brand name on a gumshield?

I checked mine when I heard about it and mine was clear – but poor Manu! I spoke to him about it and did feel very sorry for him but I saw some comments from him in the press after it happened which suggested he wasn't letting it get him down.

He was talking about how much he smiled during games, so good on him for not letting it worry him.

When you add together all the things that happened to us in New Zealand it does seem like a lot, and issues like that could have derailed the squad. It seemed at one point that anything and everything was being used against us at the World Cup. But if anything it brought us closer together and with the terrible things that are happening in the world at the moment we do need to get some sort of perspective. There are more important things to worry about.

However, those off-field issues certainly weren't in my mind in the crucial week ahead of the France game.

The day of the match flew around, the week seeming to go so fast, but again I wanted to keep the day of the match normal, like any other day. The night before every match we have a team meeting but this one was a bit different as our scrum coach Wig (Graham Rowntree) had asked to speak to us, which Johnno was fine with.

Wig gave an excellent speech. He told us he was so annoyed with the way we'd been treated and the way everyone was criticising us, when all we do is train hard and put in everything we've got.

He told us never to worry about the people who criticise us and never to get your motivation from them. Instead we should take our motivation from our friends, family and the millions of fans who were so desperate for us to do well. He reminded us that millions of people around the world would

267

be getting up at the crack of dawn, painting their faces and watching us on TV back home. They were the people to focus on and play for.

I thought it was a great message and I know all the players appreciated him saying it. He came across very well and it was exactly the right message for us.

A late kick-off is the hardest thing, because once you wake you want to get on with it. I struggle to get my head around the long days.

I had a bit of a lie-in, due to the late kick-off time. I normally stay up pretty late, so didn't get to sleep until about midnight. I don't do the same thing every evening before a match like Lewis Moody does – he goes to the cinema before each match – I try to keep things different.

Mum was with me as I had sent Melissa, with a few of the other girls, to Spookers, a haunted house attraction that the squad had been to, as we had enjoyed it so much. I spent most of my evening in the room. Mum and I just chatted, after our team meeting.

Our meal the night before is always lasagne, followed by apple pie and ice cream. This was prepared by Paulo, our amazing chef who one of our fitness guys, Calvin Morriss, found on our tour to New Zealand and Australia last summer.

Paulo was with us for almost the whole of the World Cup and the players not only loved his food but really appreciated the efforts he put in on our behalf. He was always looking to help us. He has a restaurant in Napier so had to leave us from time to time to look after that, and each time he went back to Napier the food went downhill!

After my apple pie it was time for a chat with my mum. It was great to spend a bit of time with her to talk about anything but rugby.

The day of a late kick-off is about dragging everything out for me. I try to make everything I have to do last twice as long. I got up at 10.30 on the day of the match, having slept until about 10am, which is usually an indication that I'm pretty relaxed and not stressed out. There are quite a lot of lads who sleep in for longer. Fodes would sleep until 4pm if he could.

For breakfast I had my normal omelette and porridge. All I tried to do was stick to what I'd normally eat on any other day, not making any exceptions for a game day. I managed to drag breakfast out for forty-five minutes, sitting with Hask (James Haskell). We talked about rugby and life in general. We didn't get into the detail of the game plans or tactics, as it wasn't really the right place.

At noon we made the fifteen-minute journey to Eden Park for our walk-throughs. In other words, you walk around the pitch and go through a few moves.

After that it was time for lunch, although that was quite light as there was a pre-match meal to come. For lunch I was still trying to eat some carbohydrates for the match and as usual I saved myself for the pre-match, before taking on Courtney at table tennis. Courts is good but he can't beat me!

Splashdown

After that it was back up to the room, with the objective of killing even more time before the big game.

In Cardiff for the Six Nations I went out into the streets around the hotel for sushi but at the World Cup I felt I couldn't go out like that because of all the trouble that has been caused, from nothing, so on this day I decided it was better to stay in. I felt everything cramped in on us off the pitch. Although I expected some of that as we were at a World Cup, there was so much loaded on our backs that I felt by the end I couldn't do normal things, in case they were taken the wrong way. Someone somewhere will make you look bad. Usually I do what I want to on a trip like this but for the final few weeks I couldn't be myself because of that pressure.

But no one could stop me having my favourite pre-match meal before the France game: tuna sandwiches alongside some spaghetti bolognese. By 4pm I was starting to think about the match. At this pre-match meal there's a lot less chat among the boys as we start to get more serious about what's ahead, and our 6.30pm departure time from the hotel gets closer and closer.

That meal ran almost until we set off, so it was a lot more staggered. I went in early, as I hadn't eaten since lunch and this time I added a few pancakes to my plate as well. That's all Fodes eats at this meal – he gets in there, eats pancakes and syrup and a glass of milk and goes back to bed – job done! He hardly eats anything during the day either. I'm not sure how he does it!

At this stage I'm not really thinking about my opposite number or what France will do. I've done my analysis earlier in the week and this time, a few hours before the match, is about me and what I have to do in this World Cup quarter-final and what I have to do right. I am focusing on the basics, getting those right, as I know if they're spot on then the other parts to my game will follow naturally.

After the pre-match meal I headed to my room to get my kit together, as Melissa and my mum had already headed off to the ground. There wasn't much in my bag as all the kit had been taken to the ground by our kit man, Dave 'Reg' Tennison. My boots were in my bag and it seems, after a day of the hours ticking by slowly, I was now in a rush as the time flew by to 6.30pm, when we had to get our bags on the bus.

I like to be on my own at this time, collecting my thoughts. I normally sit next to Hask on the bus as he watches a DVD on the journey to the ground, on his iPad. He will watch highlights of the best blindsides and opensides in the world – edited highlights that have been put together for him. He'll also watch some of himself playing well to give him confidence. I don't know if he's embarrassed by these videos but he always seems to seek me out as I know about them.

But this time, as Hask was taking up two seats, Mike Tindall came to sit next to me. 'It's always a good omen when I sit next to you,' he said, so I said: 'Sit down, big Mike.' It's the whole playing squad of thirty and all the management and almost every player has headphones on.

You could see Tins was desperate to play as he had a lot of energy, but you could also see he was desperate to be a good influence on the team. Tins would never throw his toys out of the pram; he always wants what's best for the team.

I like the bus trip to Eden Park, especially when the streets are packed. The route took us along the Fan Trail, which was set up to help people walk from downtown Auckland to the ground. People were standing outside the bars, many in fancy dress, and it was creating a great atmosphere in the city, pretty much exactly the same as Twickenham.

We got to the ground at around 7pm, two hours before kick-off, and the next big job was for the players to get strapped. I don't really like strapping and that night it looked like Moodos' body was being held together by strapping because there was so much of it on him. Knees, shoulders, wrists, elbows – he just seemed connected by tape. So if you do need strapping, you don't get in the queue behind Moodos.

So while everyone else was being strapped I just sat down, next to Manu and Fodes. Manu was listening to music and dancing around a little bit. We were looking at the programme, discussing some ridiculous photograph of someone. We normally do 'Spot the Difference' at Northampton, but we couldn't find anything like that in the World Cup programmes.

Then it was time to put on my new boots, which have CJA (my initials) and KTA (my dad's initials) embroidered on each side.

I checked that Reg had ironed my shorts. After the first game I noticed my shorts had a crease down the middle so I told him I couldn't have that. He obliged from then on and they looked more the part this time. I offered to take my shorts early so I could iron them, but in the end he took charge of the job.

Before the Georgia game Reg even left me a note, which I've kept, and it read: 'Here's to Ashy, England's try-scoring machine. Here's your ironed shorts – hope you are happy with no creases. Grab a handful today.' And ever since he has ironed the shorts – and they were working up until the France game.

Me and my ironed shorts then went out for my personal warm-up, and once that was over we came back in to meet the coaches.

I try to keep this personal warm-up of mine the same each time, so I start off by running around. I did a bit of kicking to myself, some stretching. Usually we would speak to Johnno once we get back in but this one was different as we went straight out this time to do the team warm-up.

Once I was back in, it was time to disappear into the toilet cubicle and have a word with my dad. I told him I hoped he was watching and that it all went well. It's important for me to have a little word before I go back out ahead of the one-minute call from the officials.

Back in the dressing room, it was shirts on and away we go after captain Moodos spoke to us. Again he spoke very well, reminding us that you don't get many chances like this in a lifetime so they have to be taken with both hands.

On the pitch we were quickly behind. It was so frustrating because there was no point in the game when I didn't feel we could take them and looking back I still feel that. That is why I've taken the defeat so hard and why I still can't come to terms with losing that match.

I kept saying to Fodes during the game, 'The French aren't that good. What are we doing?' And at the end of the game he came over to me and said, 'I can't believe this.'

The first try was absolutely schoolboy, and we were all so disappointed to have conceded such a bad try. We were all on the floor like skittles as Vincent Clerc scored.

The sort of confusion that led to that try is something that will happen once a year, so we didn't think too much of it. We also suffered from giving away too many penalties, which was one of the features of this World Cup.

We always knew we could get back into the match and that happened with two tries in the second half. At half-time we all felt we could still win the game, despite trailing 16–0. The belief was there and although Fodes went over early in the second half we couldn't follow it up until Cuets scored very late on, when it was almost too late.

Even until five minutes to go I believed we'd win. I never felt it was slipping through our hands and when we gave that penalty away with almost the final move of the match to confirm our exit I could barely believe it. We were out of the World Cup.

England 12 France 19

England

Tries: Foden, Cueto **Con:** Wilkinson
B Foden; C Ashton, M Tuilagi, T Flood, M Cueto;
J Wilkinson, B Youngs; M Stevens, S Thompson, D Cole,
L Deacon, T Palmer, T Croft, L Moody (capt), N Easter
Replacements: M Banahan for Wilkinson (65),
R Wigglesworth for Youngs (65), A Corbisiero for Stevens
(50), D Hartley for Thompson (56), M Stevens for Cole
(63), S Shaw for Deacon (50), C Lawes for Croft (47),
J Haskell for Moody (63)

France

Tries: Clerc, Medard **Pens:** Yachvili 2 **Drop-goal:** Trinh-Duc
M Medard; V Clerc, A Rougerie, M Mermoz, A Palisson;
M Parra, D Yachvili; J Poux, W Servat, N Mas, P Pape,
L Nallet, T Dusautoir (capt), J Bonnaire, I Harinordoquy
Replacements: D Marty for Rougerie (68), C Heymans for
Mermoz (79), F Trinh-Duc for Yachvili (53), F Barcella for
Poux (56), D Szarzewski for Servat (53), J Pierre for Pape (65),
L Picamoles for Harinordoquy (74)

Attendance: 49,105
Referee: S Walsh (Australia)

Splashdown

The day after the match was another long one, one of the longest of my life, which I spent at our hotel in central Auckland – a very sad day. 'It doesn't feel like I've woken up yet,' I told Melissa, about five times.

When we came back to the hotel on Saturday night people were clapping us through, but if I'm honest I'd rather have had eggs thrown at me. I didn't think I'd be able to sleep, but after some time with my family and a couple of hours lying awake in my bed I eventually dropped off, although it was a hard night.

I was sorry it had to end this way, especially for those guys who may never play for England again.

There is so much talent in this team and it hasn't been used in the right way. The most frustrating thing is that we weren't able to get the best out of each other. Hopefully this will get fixed and we can turn the corner.

We heard later that Manu had ended the World Cup by jumping off a ferry, for a swim, on his return from Waiheke Island, for which he was fined £3,000. Lucky for me I wasn't there with him as I would have jumped in with him. We started the World Cup in Auckland harbour, enjoying a trip out on one of the America's Cup boats . . . I might have ended it the same way!

But I must remember that it wasn't all doom and gloom and I have some great memories of my time with the lads in New Zealand. It's hard to say if I'm a better player for my experience but I will – as Moodos told us – do everything in my power to use the pain and the hurt to make me a better player.

I can be thankful I'm twenty-four and hopefully this won't be my last World Cup. I will use my experiences as a turning point in my rugby career . . . roll on 2015!

Epilogue

I started my amazing year in an England shirt, exactly as I wanted to, at Twickenham playing for my country against the All Blacks and then scoring a length of the field try against Australia. But I certainly didn't end it as I had planned, sitting at home on my sofa watching that same New Zealand side lift the Webb Ellis Cup.

I watched the final before heading down to Wembley for the NFL and it was, in many ways, a typical final: tight and the only surprise was that it created two tries, especially one from a prop and another from a back-rower.

You rarely get an awful lot of action out of a final. No one wants to make a mistake, no one wants to put a foot wrong and that takes over in a final.

I did struggle to watch it but it wasn't as bad as the semis which were very hard to watch. As the days went on after getting home from the World Cup it got easier but they were still difficult to watch, knowing France, who beat us, got there.

Splashdown

I don't think France were at their best when they played us, and they were a completely different team in the final. People always say you don't know which France team will turn up, but in the final it was the old France we all know, and they could easily have won it. It was better for the game as a whole to see France put up a good fight. They did a great job disrupting the All Blacks.

The story of the New Zealand half-backs is ridiculous and to see Stephen Donald, their fourth-choice number 10, come on and kick the winning penalty is an amazing story.

After the match one of the first people to contact me was Reg (Tennison), the England kit man, who congratulated me on being the World Cup's leading try scorer with six, joint with France's Vincent Clerc. At least Clerc didn't score in the final to overtake me! Reg told me it was a feat not many people manage to achieve in their lifetime, and that I should be proud of it.

That was very good of him, but it is not something I have paid too much attention to.

Before France made it into that final, Wales were so unlucky, and Leigh Halfpenny's kick was ridiculously so.

Like most rugby fans, I felt desperately sorry for Wales as everyone knows that they could easily have been in that World Cup final but for a red card in the semi-final to their captain, Sam Warburton. With fourteen men that was some effort.

Wales have improved more than any other Six Nations team

and will be formidable opponents once the 2012 tournament kicks off in February. They have given their youth a chance and they've come shining through – it is a great story on their part.

I saw the Wales v France semi-final but couldn't bring myself to watch that final kick from Halfpenny. I'm not sure why but I changed channels as he was about to strike the ball, only turning back to see the score hadn't changed, and to see a replay of the kick falling just short.

As far as England is concerned I quickly realised we can't continue to keep looking back at what might have been in New Zealand. We need to move on. Considering the twelve months New Zealand has had, including the devastating Christchurch earthquake, who could begrudge them this World Cup? They put on an incredible show for the rugby public and were so friendly the whole time I was there. It is hard to deny them the joy they are now feeling.

I don't think I have ever seen a nation so obsessed with rugby as New Zealand. Rugby is at their heart and soul like football is in England. The way the supporters get behind the All Blacks is a testament to them.

The day before the final I was back on the field again for my first start in a Northampton shirt since the World Cup. I was delighted to be able to get back on the field so quickly. It was just what I needed to get over my World Cup hangover. In the days following our return from New Zealand I was devastated by the way we went out, and feeling so bad for the fans who'd made the 12,000-mile trip and watched us on TV so early in the morning.

That first game for Northampton was against the Ospreys at Bridgend's Brewery Field. It is a really old-school rugby ground and playing there after a week of training with my mates was just what I needed. It also gave me my first chance to meet some of the new players we signed over the summer. New voices are crucial to any club. We won, which was great, and as you can imagine the banter was flying around the squad.

Regrets? I regret us going out in the Rugby World Cup quarter-finals but otherwise have nothing to regret – it has all helped me gain experience and learn some lessons.

When I started my first full year as an England player I certainly didn't envisage it being such a rollercoaster affair. One thing is for certain – when you play for England and Northampton there are rarely any dull days and so it proved in the 2010–11 season.

But what I have done is learned a lot. Learned so much from defeats in places like Dublin and Auckland for England and in the Heineken Cup final for Northampton.

At the start of last season, if someone had told me that I'd score a length of the field try against Australia, two against Wales, four against Italy and go to a Rugby World Cup, I would never have believed them in a million years.

When I came to rugby union it was with the hope of being

involved with England but what's happened in such a short space of time is incredible. It has taught me that nothing is straightforward and that you must take everything as it comes.

At Northampton we ended the year without any trophies but I would defy anyone to categorise us as failures as we made the final of the Heineken Cup, after being unbeaten in the pool stages, and the semi-finals of the Aviva Premiership. Are we satisfied with that? Definitely not, but is it a platform on which this club can build? Without question it is.

Before the year really began I lost my dad as well, which made many parts of the season very difficult. He wasn't there in person in the bad times when we lost in Dublin, in that Heineken Cup final and against France in that World Cup quarter-final and more importantly he wasn't there when the good times rolled after that try against Australia, winning the Six Nations for the first time in eight years and when I scored four tries against Italy in the Six Nations. But it doesn't mean he wasn't there with me. He wouldn't have jumped up and down on any of those occasions. He would have contained his joy inside a toughened northern exterior but I know he would have been so proud.

One thing I did this year was have a secret tattoo on the inside of my left arm with the words *Carpe Diem* on it. That is what my dad always told me – seize the day, son. And as I go forward with my rugby career that is exactly what I intend to do. Of course I was devastated by the defeat at the

Splashdown

World Cup, but because of my dad and the love and support of my friends and family I have been able to pick myself up quickly, with the intention of powering ahead into the future.

The England Squad

I spent almost five consecutive months as a member of the England rugby squad in the summer and autumn of 2011, living side by side with a management team and a committed bunch of players who had only one goal. So I thought I'd pay tribute to each of the thirty men who came to New Zealand for the 2011 Rugby World Cup . . .

PROPS
Dan Cole, Leicester Tigers, 24
The self-confessed oldest twenty-four-year-old in the world who grew a Viking beard at the World Cup. He has such a dry sense of humour, which is the case with a lot of the Leicester lads. I like Coley as he's a good guy to have around. If you're ever getting carried away with anything, he'll bring you straight back down to earth. He's the enforcer in the squad if anything needs to be done.

Splashdown

Matt Stevens, Saracens, 29

I like and admire Sos (son of Swedehead) for the way he came back from a two-year ban for taking cocaine. He's very much like Lee Mears and they're best friends. I never knew the Sos from before, just the one who has played for England in 2011. He's now a changed man, I gather, and a family man who is a great guy. His return is another great story. So many athletes from varying sports never come back from drug bans, but Matt has made it back into the England team. I'm not sure I'd have made it back if I had been out of the game for two years – I'd be P&D-ing (painting and decorating) within two months. He's a hell of a wrestler too so I wouldn't go near him on the floor.

Alex Corbisiero, London Irish, 23

I call him Clark Kent because of his looks and not because he has superpowers. I also call him The Italian Baker, because he looks like one. He looks like he's been baking all his life and eating the food as well; although I've been worried about him lately as he's been losing weight. The rapper of the squad, he's an Italian-American who can rap with the best. I'm always giving him banter about his weight so in New Zealand he rapped some banter about me, mentioning my different-sized ears and other embarrassing things about me. I had nothing to come back to him with. He slaughtered me!

David Wilson, Bath Rugby, 26

Davey Bob is one of the quiet lads of the squad who doesn't do much media, just gets his head down and gets on with life. He's quiet in the outside world, but when you get to know him he's quite loud. He says some funny stuff – he's hilarious and hangs around with anyone. Most people don't notice that he has an elbow injury, which means he carries his arm like a cowboy about to draw his gun. Apparently he was doing bench presses when he was younger and the bar snapped, breaking his elbow.

Andrew Sheridan, Sale Sharks, 32

I was gutted for Shez because he only lasted one game of the World Cup as he had to go home with a shoulder injury. He's a man with a lot of skills and whenever I see him at Pennyhill Park he seems to be in the bar, with his laptop out, drinking a glass of wine. If Shez ever has some time to spare he seems to pick up a new skill. He's a qualified wine taster, bricklayer and an accomplished guitar player with his own album on iTunes. He has a CV as long as my arm.

HOOKERS

Dylan Hartley, Northampton Saints, 25

A good friend and a great skipper at the club. I spend quite a bit of time with him at Northampton. He's someone who looks like me. I call him my fatter brother and people get us mixed up a lot of the time. I hate it, because I think he is fat, but he doesn't mind it when people do mix us up. I first met him at Northampton when he was banned for gouging, and he was running the water on and off the pitch when I played my first few games for the club. It was a bit strange for him not to be playing but since then he's gone from strength to strength and it was a great move by the club to make him captain. It has made a huge difference to him as a man and to the Saints.

Steve Thompson, London Wasps, 33

Another great story, this time of a man who retired from rugby due to a serious neck injury and then paid back his insurance money to get back on the pitch. I heard he'd ballooned to around 135 kilos at one point, so he must have taken off one or two kilos – or maybe put a couple on – to get back in the England team! Seriously, to come back from retiring shows it must have meant so much to him. To get back into starting in the World Cup after that is pretty impressive. I think Tommo sees me as a young idiot and wants to put me in my place as soon as possible. You've got to have some people like that around.

Lee Mears, Bath Rugby, 32

Another one in a tough position at the World Cup as he was the third hooker, ensuring his chances were limited. But he's a guy who never stops smiling. Every time I see him he's smiling and he has a great influence around the squad. I don't think

I've ever heard him say something negative, which is pretty impressive. When you're around the same group of lads for so long your head will go at some point, but not with Lee – he's always happy, always willing to talk to any of the players about anything. A good bloke to have around.

SECOND ROW

Courtney Lawes, Northampton Saints, 22

We call him The Javelin because of the way he throws himself around the pitch. He loves a set of headphones, does Courts. He's either got them over his ears or around his neck, sometimes with his hood up. He's done remarkably well to make so much progress in such a short space of time. It doesn't seem a day ago that he was at Northampton with a hoodie under his training top, not looking interested, and now he's a regular in the England squad. He's really impressed me with his progression to where he is now: a tattooed man tackling people right, left and centre. The ladies like him, surprisingly, and he gets a lot of attention.

Louis Deacon, Leicester Tigers, 31

Another quiet member of the squad, the silent assassin. He's the hard-working grafter every team needs to be successful. Floody says every team needs a Deacs – a big, massive bloke who does his job very well and without complaint. He never says a word about it, he just keeps doing it.

Simon Shaw, Unattached, 38
Old man Shawsy was one of the best blokes in the World Cup, without a doubt. I get on with him really well. He just missed out on the 1995 World Cup, when I was eight. We have this conversation all the time, but to me he's my age. That's the way we get on – I just see him as being the same age as me. That's the way he is – he loves a joke, loves the craic and loves going out for a drink. He can't be beaten either. Everyone said he couldn't make the Lions in 2009 but he did. Everyone said he couldn't make the World Cup in 2011 but he did – remarkable! He just keeps going, like a machine.

Tom Palmer, Stade Français, 32
If you asked a girl, 'What do you want in a man looks-wise?', then I imagine they would describe Tom. I think he has all the attributes to be a woman's ideal man. He also speaks French, which is another positive. TP is tall, dark and handsome, with long hair that he's always flicking – there is so much of it. He's a great player and although he's quiet he's more than willing to open up when you talk to him.

BACK ROW
Lewis Moody, Bath Rugby, 33
Mad Dog. Exactly what it says on the tin. He throws himself into anything at 100mph, even training. His commitment levels are huge. He speaks superbly to us before games and he's the perfect captain because he goes through the brick wall first

and asks us to follow him, rather than the other way around. He's another player who's been there and done it all, so he speaks from experience, which is crucial. I always feel a little bit safer when he's playing.

Tom Croft, Leicester Tigers, 26

We like to tell Haskell he's a poor man's Tom Croft, mainly because he hates it so much. We call Tom Yog as in Yogi Bear, but I have no idea why. He's a superb athlete who is never less than outstanding on the pitch. He's very quick, especially for a forward, and he's another Lion, and one who did so well in 2009.

James Haskell, Ricoh Black Rams, 26

A very good bloke, and the player who takes the most stick from everyone else. People don't realise – because of his outward manner – that he's one of the most dedicated players in the game today. He puts a huge amount of time into his rugby. He loves the media and loves to chat a lot. He puts a lot of time into his relationships with the media and with sponsors – he's constantly looking ahead. He thinks some people have a bad impression of him, but I don't know where that comes from as he's a great guy to have around.

Nick Easter, Harlequins, 33

What to say about Minty? We call him Minty after a character in *EastEnders*. He's the worst-dressed man in the squad without a doubt. He comes into the team room some days in some horrendous clothes. Honestly, pink polo shirts and blue cardigans. He genuinely thinks he looks good too, which makes it worse. Away from his clothes I do admire him for his old-school attitude, and the moustache he grew during the World Cup proves he doesn't care what people say.

Tom Wood, Northampton Saints, 25

We always give Woody stick because he's constantly doing DIY and improving his house. We tell him he wears a tool belt whenever he's at home! He's always finding stuff to build, knock up or mend – he does all kinds of jobs. He just seems to always want a task. Whether it's hitting rucks or building a shed, he's straight on it and he won't stop until he's finished.

Thomas Waldrom, Leicester Tigers, 28

The thirty-first member of the England World Cup squad, the man they call The Tank. He's a really good player and it was good to have him with us in New Zealand. It was tough for him to come into the squad in the middle of the World Cup, but he handled it really well. I trust him to slip in and do a good job whenever he gets the chance.

HALF-BACKS

Ben Youngs, Leicester Tigers, 22

He calls me The Weasel because he reckons I'm always sticking my head up out of rucks and giving people stick. Considering his age, he's done remarkably well. He loves a bit of butter. You should see him butter his bread – he puts loads on. He loves nothing more than a big piece of bread and butter. He's obsessed with it.

Joe Simpson, London Wasps, 23

He was so happy to be at the World Cup, but it must have been frustrating for him as he didn't get too many chances to shine. The role of the third scrum-half is tough at a World Cup as chances are so limited. He has a good set of wheels but needs to shave his back hair as it's often poking over the top of his T-shirt. I was impressed with him when he came on against Georgia and he could surprise a few people when he gets a proper chance at Test level. We have to keep an eye on him when we play Wasps.

Richard Wigglesworth, Saracens, 28

Rat boy! Don't you think he looks like Roland Rat? I first got to know him on the Australia tour in 2010. He's mainly friends with Fodes and Cuets from his Sale days, but I'm becoming good friends with him now. He's another good lad but he's never shy to knock you down and put you in your place. He's always on hand to do that, but you need it. He became a father during the World Cup, which must have been hard on him as his family were at home.

Jonny Wilkinson, Toulon, 32

Mr Perfectionist. He's been amazing this year and never lets anyone down, setting new standards all the time. Jonny's career is one of the great stories, from kicking that drop-goal in 2003 to all the injuries and to finally winning his place back in the starting line-up for the 2011 World Cup. One day someone will make a film about his life. His only nickname is Wilko, although I might start calling him God.

Toby Flood, Leicester Tigers, 26

What can we say about Floody? This World Cup was hard for him, but it's always going to be when there's only one No 10 shirt on offer. He has a really good rugby brain, knows exactly what he's talking about and when he's got his chance he's done a really good job. He's always willing to help anyone out and is a big talker on the pitch – he's the one shouting and telling the lads where to go, so he performs a vital function.

CENTRES

Manu Tuilagi, Leicester Tigers, 20

I slowly got to know Manu as the World Cup campaign went on and he's a good guy. He felt more at home with the squad by the end of the World Cup, as it does take time to get to know everyone. He's a happy bloke who never means anyone any harm, but he's the shape of a car so I think if he hurts people it's by accident! He's a key part of England's future and I hope to be in the side with him for many years to come.

Every time anything gets mentioned about him punching me he just laughs – that's all I can get out of him!

Mike Tindall, Gloucester Rugby, 33

Lord Tindall, as I like to call him after his marriage to the Queen's granddaughter, Zara Phillips, earlier this year. How a man from Yorkshire gets to marry into royalty is beyond me, but it gives hope for us all! He's a great guy and ever since I came into the squad I've got on well with him and enjoyed being captained by him. He had such a hard time at the World Cup and there was nothing in it. I suppose when you marry royalty it brings that extra media attention. He handles it all very well but it's still harsh on him.

Shontayne Hape, London Irish, 30

Shapes or, to give him his proper title, DJ Shapes. He's the man you can rely on for an iPod for the bus. He's a genuinely nice guy who always has a smile and something good to say. He's never short of conversation and with his background I can always talk to him about rugby league, so we chat not only about the sport but people he knows and I know. Like a lot of Kiwis, he has a great attitude to life. I really rate him as a player too because I've played against him and watched him play for years and years. I know what he's done and maybe people in rugby union don't.

BACK THREE
Ben Foden, Northampton Saints, 26
I know a lot about my Northampton team-mate so I'd better be careful what I say! I probably spend the most time with Fodes, as we usually share a room together on England duty and on Northampton away trips. We're both from the North but we're very different, which is maybe why we get on so well. His girlfriend is Una Healy from The Saturdays – he fancies himself as a pop star. On the pitch he's someone I talk to a lot. He says I moan a lot during games, which is probably right. He's very messy when we share a room, and doesn't have a care in the world. I'd tell him if I had a problem in my private life, but I don't think he'd do the same with me. He thinks I'd tell everyone, which is probably right!

Delon Armitage, London Irish, 27
He loves to think he's the bad lad but he isn't really. He likes to think he's the hard man. His teeth are amazing. Until recently he still had kids' milk teeth and he had them veneered so he looks like the bloke out of *There's Something About Mary*. He has the biggest and best smile in the squad, with his set of shiny teeth. He goes around smiling all the time.

Mark Cueto, Sale Sharks, 31
The old man of the back three and someone who's been a huge help to me. Since I've come into the England squad, he's always been there to help me out, as we've been part of one of

the most-capped back three – as a unit – in England's history. I change next to him at Twickenham. It was hard on him at the World Cup as his back problem made him miss some games, although he did finish the tournament with a try – not that that will be any consolation for him. I call him The Old Conker Tree, as he's so experienced. It's something we used to say in Wigan – if you cut a conker tree open they have loads of rings showing their age, so if you cut Cuets open there would be loads of rings in there. And also conker trees live for hundreds of years.

Matt Banahan, Bath Rugby, 24

You don't get what you see on the tin with Matt as he's 6ft 7in and covered in tattoos, yet is one of the nicest guys you'll ever meet. He's a gentle giant, so if you get to know him you won't regret it because he's a top bloke. He has recently started a family, which has changed his life to a certain extent. He's calmed down a little bit.

Acknowledgements

No project like this could be completed without the love and support of my family – Mum, Claire, Beth and David (Trev) alongside my far better other half – Melissa! And of course all the players involved. Thanks also go to Paul Morgan, the editor of *Rugby World* magazine with whom I collaborated on the book, Simon Mills at the RFU, Chris Wearmouth at Northampton, my managers Andi Peters and Andy Clarke, Kerr MacRae at Simon & Schuster . . . and last but definitely not least Rhea Halford at Simon & Schuster for her wise counsel and superb editing skills. I hope you enjoy the book!

Picture Credits

Section 1

Page 1: Getty Images, Getty Images, Getty Images, Getty Images

Page 2: Getty Images, Richard Lane

Page 3: Getty Images, Getty Images

Page 4: TopFoto, Rex Features, TopFoto

Page 5: Getty Images, Getty Images

Page 6: Getty Images, Getty Images, Getty Images, Getty Images

Page 7: Action Images, Action Plus, Action Plus

Page 8: Getty Images, Getty Images, Getty Images, Getty Images

Section 2

Page 1: Getty Images, Getty Images, Getty Images

Page 2: Getty Images, Getty Images, Action Images

Page 3: Getty Images, Action Images, Getty Images